Australian Biographical Monographs

18

Australian Biographical Monographs

Series Editor: Scott Prasser

Previous Volumes

Robert (Bob) Hawke	Mike Steketee
John Curtin	David Lee
Jack Lang	David Clune
Leonie Kramer	Damien Freeman
Margaret Guilfoyle	Anne Henderson
William McKell	David Clune
Neville Bonner	Sean Jacobs
George Reid	Luke Walker
Robert Askin	Paul Loughnan
John Grey Gorton	Paul Williams
Stanley Melbourne Bruce	David Lee
Robert Menzies	Scott Prasser
Neville Wran	David Clune
Lindsay Thompson	William Westerman
Johannes Bjelke-Petersen	Bruce Kingston
Harold Holt	Tom Frame
Joseph Lyons	Kevin Andrews

Australian Biographical Monographs

18

Annabelle Rankin

Peter Sekuless

Connor Court Publishing

Australian Biographical Monographs 18

Annabelle Rankin by Peter Sekuless
Published in 2023 by Connor Court Publishing Pty Ltd

Copyright © Peter Sekuless

All rights reserved. No part of this book may be reproduced or transmitted in any form or by any means, electronic or mechanical, including photo copying, recording or by any information storage and retrieval system, without prior permission in writing from the publisher.

Connor Court Publishing Pty Ltd
PO Box 7257
Redland Bay QLD 4165
sales@connorcourt.com
www.connorcourt.com
Phone 0497-900-685

Printed in Australia

ISBN: 9781922815385

Front Cover Photograph from album maintained by Dame Annabelle Jane Mary Rankin DBE - Annabelle Rankin at Parliament House in Canberra in 1946. Series/Control symbol, M2127, 1, Item ID 8847383, National Archives of Australia, Canberra.

I'm a very ordinary, everyday sort of person. I did not set out to do any of these things. The war came and it changed a lot of lives, especially mine. The opportunities came along. I love hard work and one thing led to another. It's a matter of recognising the opportunity and grabbing it. Nothing was given to me easily. I had to justify every appointment I have received.
- Dame Annabelle Rankin, 1981.

Series overview

Connor Court's Australian Biographical Series on past Australian political leaders and other important figures seeks to provide an overview for those who are unfamiliar with the subject and to highlight the person's particular importance, controversies around them, and their contributions to Australia's progress.

The monographs are scholarly rather than academic in focus, placing emphasis on a clear narrative, but with careful attention to referencing to ensure views expressed are supported by appropriate sources and evidence.

The Series was initiated because of the decline in the study of Australian history at our schools and universities. Consequently, there has been a lack of knowledge or, even worse, distorted views, of some of Australia's leading historical figures who deserve to be remembered, better understood for their achievements, and, as each volume also highlights, their flaws.

This is the first biography of Dame Annabelle Rankin since 1981. Dame Annabelle was a Liberal Senator from Queensland from 1947-71. This monograph is a timely reminder of her many achievements. She heralded many firsts. She was the first woman Senator from Queensland, the first woman to become Whip of any party in Federal Parliament, the first woman with ministerial responsibility for a government department, and the first to head a diplomatic mission when appointed High Commissioner to New Zealand. As Government Whip in the Senate Rankin showed how its legislation could get passed even when the Coalition Government did not have a Senate majority. As Minister for Housing Rankin brought a new caring focus to the Coalition Government's housing policies as well as promoting its traditional policy of increasing levels of home ownership. Most importantly, as her tireless visits to all parts of Australia highlighted, Senator Rankin never forgot that elected officials are there to serve the people and that it is essential they understand people's needs and their conditions. This was not limited to her native Queensland but took her to many parts of urban Australia to see how elderly pensioners and others really lived.

Peter Sekuless has brought Dame Annabelle to life in this meticulously researched monograph. He has made extensive use of parliamentary debates, contemporary press reports, and most importantly, interviews recorded after Senator Rankin's retirement. We are all the more informed not just about Dame Annabelle, but of the culture and values of the times in which she lived and the prejudices that she, and others like her, had to overcome. Her story also tells us a lot about the Commonwealth Parliament itself and the nature of the Liberal Party which was perhaps more of a pioneer in women's rights than is usually acknowledged.

Peter Sekuless is an author who has written on a variety of subjects including Australian women who have battled against the odds. His first book was a biography of a prominent feminist, *Jessie Street: A rewarding but unrewarded life* published in 1978. *In A Handful of Hacks* (1999), he wrote of the achievements of the journalist Lorraine Stumm who reported on World War Two in New Guinea and the Pacific. In chronological order, he has been a daily newspaper journalist, a Commonwealth public servant and a Canberra lobbyist.

■   Scott Prasser (Series Editor)

Foreword

When the editor of this series of biographical monographs Dr Scott Prasser signalled he wanted to add Dame Annabelle Rankin to the series, I soon became an enthusiastic contender to record her pioneering contribution to Australian history.

Dame Annabelle has been overlooked for too long. As Minister for Housing in the Holt and Gorton Governments, she was the first woman with responsibility for a federal government department and as High Commissioner to New Zealand was the first woman to head an Australian diplomatic post. She was, too, the first female whip in the Australian Parliament.

As a young journalist in the Canberra press gallery in the late 1960s I had observed Dame Annabelle in the Senate chamber of Old Parliament House. I was seeing her at the height of her political career as Minister for Housing, having been a Senator occupying her place in the beautifully proportioned, red-upholstered, red-carpeted Senate chamber for more than two decades. She had first entered that chamber as a new Senator for Queensland in 1947 and it had been her place of work ever since.

In fact, I was only in Canberra at all thanks to Dame Annabelle. As a school boy in my last year of school, I had been taken to her office in Brisbane for an interview with her. I had shown an interest in public and government affairs as a career and she suggested a good starting point would be a degree from the Australian National University in Canberra.

Her office in the Commonwealth parliamentary building adjacent to the always verdant and beautifully maintained Anzac Square was her other place of work. Members of Parliament have two offices, one in Parliament House and the other in their electorate. Senator Rankin's electorate was the whole of Queensland and she cultivated it assiduously, using her Brisbane office as the base from which she maintained contact with an extensive range of individuals and organisations throughout the State.

I followed in her footsteps from Brisbane to Canberra a decade and a half after her and, by chance, came to know first-hand the spaces she occupied in work and leisure. I can instinctively slip into the rhythm of her life as a Senator revolving around Question Time after lunch on each sitting day, the weekly party meetings and meals in the parliamentary refreshment rooms served by waitresses in starched white uniforms.

To revive knowledge of her life and achievements by writing this biographical monograph is a privilege.

Introduction

Senator for Queensland, Government Whip, Minister for Housing, High Commissioner to New Zealand, Dame of the British Empire, Annabelle Rankin was one of the most successful politicians of her era. She outperformed and outlasted most of her male and all her female contemporaries thanks to hard work and persistence. Her most significant achievements were to be the first woman to represent Queensland in the Senate, the first woman to be a Government Whip in both the Australian Parliament and the British Commonwealth, first woman Minister of the Crown with responsibility for a government department and first woman to represent Australia as a diplomat of ambassadorial rank.

Annabelle Rankin was not alone in achieving multiple firsts. The same can be said of the other five members of the cohort of six women pioneers who won their way into the national Parliament in the 1940s; two each at the successive 1943, 1946 and 1949 federal elections. Dorothy Tangney whose career most closely parallels Rankin's became the first woman Senator and first woman to represent both Western Australia and the Australian Labor Party (ALP) when she was elected in 1943, three years before Rankin. They were born but a year apart, Tangney in 1907, Rankin in 1908.

Annabelle – who became universally known by her first name – succeeded in becoming a Minister, but not the more senior rank of Cabinet Minister, in the period when Sir Robert Menzies and Harold Holt were prime ministers from 1949 to 1967. A prominent feature of both administrations was that they favoured continuity over renewal with new ministerial appointments. So sparing was Menzies in promoting the considerable backbench talent which entered Parliament after the Second World War that many who did not make it to the front bench abandoned the struggle.

Although breaking with some of Menzies' precedents, Holt was similarly economical with appointing new ministers. Following his only general election success in 1966 he made a mere two changes to the ministry he had inherited. One of those appointments was Senator Dame Annabelle Rankin as Minister for Housing; the other was Malcolm Fraser. Rankin had demonstrated a persistence not shared by some male colleagues who had left Parliament. She had built an enviable reputation over a decade and a half as an effective, hard-working Government Senate Whip.

She succeeded in making the all-important move to which politicians aspire, promotion to the frontbench as a minister of the crown. And there she stayed through the term of John Gorton's prime ministership until 1971, when her career in public life was crowned with a diplomatic posting as High Commissioner to New Zealand.

Annabelle was one of many prominent members of the

Menzies and post-Menzies governments whose record of 23 years in power still stands but in relation to other women she was first among equals. Rankin stands out for her length of service and the ministerial and diplomatic ranks she attained. She was the most successful of the high achieving '40s sextet who together were a microcosm of the nation geographically, politically, socio-economically, and importantly at the time religiously. They were also noteworthy numerically. The six did not sit in the Parliament at the same time as one lost her seat in the 1949 election. This meant that with the two new women Senators from that election, there were five female representatives at the opening of Parliament in 1950 which ushered in the new Liberal-Country Party era.

A decade later, in 1960, the number of female representatives remained the same at five but had changed into a less diverse group. The 1960s cohort were all in the Senate. The two members of the House of Representatives were not replaced when one retired and the other lost her seat. After Rankin resigned in 1971, the number of women parliamentarians had dropped to two, both Senators.

By 1975 the total number of women elected to Parliament since 1943 was still only 14 including the original six from the 1940s. The rate of increase in female representation slowed in the 1950s and 1960s before picking up in the

1970s mostly due to the advent of ALP women.

By comparison the arrival of two new women in three successive elections in the 1940s was a high point of women's representation. Along with Annabelle and Dorothy Tangney they included the Tasmanian Enid Lyons, then of the United Australia Party, who in 1943 became the first woman elected to the House of Representatives. In 1946 Doris Blackburn from Victoria became the second woman and first Independent elected to the House. In 1949, two new woman Senators, Ivy Wedgewood from Victoria and Agnes Robertson from Western Australia, both Liberals, were elected.

Each of these women had broken barriers and set precedents to represent their sex in the Australian Parliament. In her roles, first as a Whip and then as a Minister, Annabelle had achieved most on the political front. Under the prime ministerships of Sir Robert Menzies, Harold Holt and John Gorton, she was to become the most successful woman in the Liberal Party and in federal politics. Her standing was not matched until another Liberal woman, Senator Margaret Guilfoyle, became a Cabinet Minister in 1976.[1]

But half a century later when women's representation, particularly in the Liberal Party, has become a political and election issue of some significance few can recall the name and fewer the achievements of Dame Annabelle Rankin. One of the few memorials to her is a Queensland electorate bearing her name. Following the 2022 federal election the Member for Rankin, Jim Chalmers, became Treasurer in the victorious Albanese Labor Government.

Annabelle's legacy includes paving the way for two notable successors. After she resigned to become High Commissioner to New Zealand in 1971, her replacement in the Senate was Neville Bonner,[2] the first Aboriginal Australian to enter the national parliament. Three years later, another woman chosen by the Queensland branch of the Liberal Party to stand for the Senate, described Annabelle as "my greatest help". This was Kathy Martin Sullivan who became the first woman to serve both in the Senate and the House of Representatives.

In the 1970s Kathy Martin Sullivan found the challenges of dealing with an electorate still sceptical of women's abilities were not replicated in the Senate itself where, she said, "It was just like being a male Senator". As she went on to explain:

> Most likely, the memory of Dame Annabelle Rankin, having been both a Whip of many years standing and a Minister ... meant that the men were used to working not only with women, but with women who were in a position of authority – an experience totally atypical of Australian society in those days.[3]

Early life and the war years

Much of Annabelle Rankin's life was dictated by politics. Even her place of birth was decided by parliamentary schedule, in this case the Queensland Legislative Assembly. Although her family lived 300 kilometres to the north she was born in Brisbane as her father, Colonel Colin Rankin, was the state Member for Burrum which covered the area where the family lived. Annabelle was born on 28 July 1908 and named after her mother. She was the Rankins' first child. A second daughter, Jean, was born in 1914.

The sisters were born into a life of considerable privilege. Colonel Rankin was the third successive member of his family to be managing director of The Queensland Collieries Company Limited. The London-based corporation owned and operated mines in the coal field around Howard, north west of Maryborough in the Wide Bay district of the state, now better known as the Fraser Coast. It was the largest coal mining operation in that locality. The family home named Brooklyn House was the most imposing residence in the town. For much of the current century it has been a tourist attraction in the historic town of Howard. It has now reverted to being a private residence.[4]

The citation for heritage significance under the Queensland Heritage Act for Brooklyn House provides a precise description of the place the Rankin family occupied at the time. The family had been the most prominent in the district from the mid-1880s when Annabelle's grandfather, William Rankin, was appointed to manage the mining operation, until 1940 when her father died.

The Heritage Register states:

> Brooklyn House is important in demonstrating the principal characteristics of a wealthy colonial residence in the region, in particular, the spatial relationship between the House and St Matthews Church next door and how this reflected the wealth and importance of the Rankin family in Howard.[5]

Under the section for historical context, the register describes the House as being the centrepiece of social life in Howard. It was built for William Rankin by a local carpenter in 1890, six years after he had arrived from Scotland to manager of the British-owned coal mine:

> Originally set on three acres of land with gardens, formal drives, bowling green and tennis court. A gate connected the garden to the local Anglican churchyard next door.[6]

Brooklyn House was not Annabelle's home for the first years of her life. She lived on a sugar farm 30 kilometres inland from Howard near Childers. Annabelle's father Colin was a mining engineer like his father and had worked at Queensland Collieries from its inception. He branched out on his own as a sugar farmer and politician after returning from the Boer War via the United Kingdom where he had been evacuated to recover from war wounds.

During the First World War Colin was again away from Australia when his father died. A brother, Charles, took over management of the mines but died two years later in 1919. Colin Rankin and his family moved from Childers to Howard to take over management of the colliery and live in Brooklyn House. Annabelle was old enough to remember the disruption of moving quite clearly. Her recollections are of taking a large collection of pets – dog, cat, parrot and pony – by train to their new home.[7]

Of more relevance to her later political career is a family memory of her childhood in Childers. Annabelle's mother was amused by her elder daughter imitating her father making speeches replete with appropriate gestures. Annabelle herself frequently repeated this anecdote in speeches of her own and in interviews to describe her early interest in public life. She recalled:

> He (her father) had, I think, an unknown and unknowing influence on me because when I was quite a small child I used to play at being a member of parliament. I would play that I was opening fetes and all that sort of thing and making speeches.[8]

Annabelle's childhood in the small town of Howard was largely confined to the church next door and school nearby. Her greatest problem was the propensity of Trixie, her pony, to steal the school lunches of other pupils. With loving and protective parents, life was isolated but happy. Her horizon widened when she was sent to board at Glennie Memorial School for her secondary schooling.

Glennie was a Church of England girls school in Toowoomba, west of Brisbane. She remembered her time at Glennie fondly and Glennie has remembered her. A portrait of her in evening dress with long gloves and her medals hangs in pride of place. There is also an annual award named after her. Her record at school was not outstanding but she did become a prefect in her final year.[9] Much later, when she was in a similar position of responsibility over her peers in the Senate, a fellow female Liberal Senator accused her of wielding her authority like a "head prefect", a promotion Annabelle never achieved at school.[10]

In the next phase of her life Annabelle began to make connections with organisations which would underpin her political career, although that was not her intention at the time. She returned to Howard and undertook the voluntarily work appropriate for her class and her family's place in society, more suitable at the time as a preparation for marriage than a preparation for life in politics or the workforce. Her activities mostly involved the church, such as Sunday School teaching, but it was her role in establishing and leading a local Girl Guide group which pointed the way forward. Statewide organisations including the Girl Guides, Young Women's Christian Association, Country Women's Association and Red Cross supported her strongly throughout her political career, delivering her a significant personal vote at successive Senate elections.

Then came her grand overseas tour. Thanks to her father who believed young people should see the world this was more than the obligatory trip "home". She went to China and Japan as well as Europe and the United Kingdom. As a result, she was more aware of gathering war clouds than most Australians. In Shanghai, she saw the damage aerial bombing does to cities. Then, she chanced to be in Gibraltar and saw another city in flames from bombardment across the isthmus in Spain in that country's Civil War. In England she met a cousin involved in the settlement of refugees from the Spanish war.

Annabelle was back home when the Second World War came to Australia. The Rankin family were at their beach house near Maryborough with a group of young people to hear then Prime Minister Robert Menzies make his melancholy announcement on the wireless that Australia was at war. Forty years later she had a poignant memory of that moment, telling her biographer, Waveney Browne:

> My father, an old soldier, understood what those words meant, but all of us who were young

> probably did not. When I look back on that group, my sister and I and one other are the only ones left. All the others paid the supreme sacrifice and somehow that to me is a breathtaking experience. I think of what those young people could have contributed to the world and I am so grateful to them for making the sacrifice and giving us the freedom we now enjoy.[11]

The war also brought Annabelle the opportunities which led directly to her becoming a Senator. She quite literally went from being in uniform to election campaigning. The intervening years brought dramatic change to Queensland and Queenslanders. The extent of the change for the women involved is well described by Rupert Goodman in his book on Queensland military nurses:

> In the second half of 1942 Queensland was virtually an armed camp, from Warwick and Toowoomba on the Darling Downs through to Thursday Island in the north. As camps developed, so the medical services had to be provided. Queensland Line of Communication Area or QL of C as it became known encompassed a massive army organisation controlling the troops and their movement in Queensland.[12]

Women's organisations were formally attached to the armed services to cope with the build-up of both Australian and American troops. Annabelle's former school, Glennie, and Downlands, a boys school in Toowoomba were taken over by the Army and became military hospitals.

Other existing elements of civil society were co-opted, and willingly so, into military organisations with a bewildering array of acronyms including AWAS (Australian Women's Army Service), Voluntary Aid Detachments (VAD) and AAMWS (Australian Army Medical Women's Service). Both Rankin sisters worked for these organisations, Jean as a nursing sister and Lieutenant in the AAMWS and Annabelle as initially a blue-uniformed VAD and later in khaki in the AWAS. In recognition of her war service, Annabelle was awarded the War Medal 1939-45 and the Australian Service Medal 1939-45, both of which she wore with pride whenever the occasion required.

With the death of her father in 1940 Annabelle moved to Brisbane and began paid work for the first time as a clerk in a trustee company. In the evenings she became a member of a Voluntary Aid Detachment set up by the Girl Guides. In the early 'phoney war' period the tasks were preparatory and routine such as staffing air raid shelters and hospital support work. She was stationed at the air raid shelter in the Customs House on Queen Street, her tasks confined mainly to filling up hurricane lamps for lighting with fuel at the start of an alert and emptying them after the "all clear".

Early in 1942 Annabelle was appointed as State Secretary of the Queensland Girl Guides Association. A little over a year later the Girl Guides released her for urgent work with the Army through the Young Women's Christian Association. As Assistant Commissioner of the YWCA War Services for Queensland and northern New South Wales she became directly involved in war work. She was responsible for the welfare services for service women. The YWCA was well placed to provide these with its network of hostels providing places of rest and relaxation for women on leave from New Guinea and further afield as the Japanese were pushed back.

In addition to her welfare responsibilities Annabelle was called on to escort VIP visitors around Queensland and on occasion New Guinea. These included the wife of the President of the United States, Eleanor Roosevelt, and the wife of the Australian Governor-General, Lady Gowrie. Her travels around the State both on escort duty and tours to inspect the welfare facilities for service women were good practice for her life to come as a Senator whose electorate was the whole of Queensland. Lady Gowrie, in particular, proved to be good company. The accommodation for their visit to the Atherton Tablelands was the same as that used by the Australian Army commander-in-chief General Blamey. Lady Gowrie was highly amused because her husband, the Governor-General Lord Gowrie, frequently clashed with General Blamey.

Public relations was part of her Army role and from

time to time she was required to address civilian meetings to inform people on what was being done for servicewomen. Part of her role was to solicit public support for activities such as donating items of home comfort to make rest houses more welcoming for service women on leave. It was at one of those meetings towards the end of the war that Annabelle impressed lawyer Charles Wanstall, an executive member of the Queensland People's Party (QPP) and member of the Queensland Legislative Assembly. Wanstall, later Chief Justice of Queensland, told the ABC, that he had met Annabelle when she was still in the services towards the end of 1945. He said:

> She was guest speaker at an annual meeting at which I was present. I was so impressed by her demeanour and what she had to say, I suggested she might like to put her name in for a selection panel for a Senate election when one was coming up in a few months.[13]

Assistant Commissioner Rankin who made such a good impression on Wanstall at the end of the war was a far remove from the pre-war Annabelle Rankin, a young woman of good family but with no qualifications and little life experience. The more mature woman standing and speaking before an audience that night looked and sounded like a person capable of accepting and exercising responsibility. Dressed in an army uniform and wearing the shoulder tabs of an officer, Annabelle was "a find".[14]

At that time both Charles Wanstall and Annabelle Rankin were weighing crucial decisions about the future.

Wanstall was one of the young professionals active in the QPP which was established to replace the defunct United Australia Party in the northern state in 1943. Another professional with political ambitions was Dr Winston Noble who became a State MLA in 1950 and later Health Minister. At the urging of the Liberal Party organiser in Queensland, Charles Porter, they were attracted to merging with the new Liberal Party as other successors to the United Australia Party were doing elsewhere but they were conscious that the old guard of the QPP was jealously guarding their party's independence.

The new guard was very aware that their party needed to change if it was to challenge the predominant position the Country Party occupied in terms of national representation. Artie Fadden was clearly the senior Queensland politician nationally in the House of Representatives and the experienced Senator Walter Cooper was firmly at the top of the joint Senate team.

The question of women's representation and the need to attract women's votes was also a consideration. Porter, the political professional, stressed the importance of the women's vote in terms of numbers. There were more women than men voters in Queensland particularly in the south east where the Liberals and QPP were strongest. The new federal Liberal leader Robert Menzies regularly addressed the importance of women and women's issues. This was partly due to the influence of the Australian Women's National League, and partly to political tactics.

In the national 1946 campaign the Liberal Party targeted both women's issues and the role of women more generally. This was a point of difference from the Labor Party which was firmly in power following its own electoral success in 1943 and which had little to fear from its opponents, the recently cobbled-together Liberal Party.

One of the few bright spots for the Opposition was the 1943 election of Enid Lyons. As the first woman elected to the House of Representatives, she attracted national publicity and was a considerable asset to a dispirited and divided opposition. Although Lyons' success was attributed by some to riding on her late husband's coat tails, her effectiveness and prominence as a member of the Opposition team once she arrived in Canberra as a Member of the lower house in her own right was obvious to all. Annabelle owed much to Enid Lyons, who was to become her mentor in due course and paved the way by example for her selection as a Senate candidate.

Enid Lyons also became a rare confidant. In the ABC's tribute to Annabelle, Lyons said, "My impression is that she didn't want to lead other than a single life because she had once been engaged to be married, I think, and her fiancée had died."[15]

During her first election campaign and early political career Rankin resolutely refused to explain why she remained single. If her fiancée had been killed in the war, as she told another trusted confidant, she obviously had a strong desire for this to remain a private memory.[16] It could however help explain her deep reverence for former servicemen among her future colleagues, particularly those such as John Gorton, wounded when the plane he was piloting was shot down, and Justin O'Byrne who had been a POW of the Germans.

In 1946, the QPP selectors had much to weigh up when selecting the Liberal Senate candidates and not least the claim of the incumbent Senator Harry Foll, a former minister who was seeking re-endorsement.

The considerations facing Annabelle were entirely different. The end of the war would mean that her Army job would no longer exist. A job back with the Girl Guides was on offer but it involved running the junior branch of the guides which was a lesser role than that she had left nearly three years before. More tempting was a role with the United Nations Relief and Rehabilitation Authority in Greece. When the approach to stand for Senate selection came, the choices for Annabelle were between settling for a backwards step by confirming the junior Girl Guides position, moving into the future either overseas with the United Nations in Europe or a possible political role which would involve a move to Canberra.

Wanstall had actively encouraged her to stand for Senate pre-selection although she was not a party member at the time. Recalling her reaction to Wanstall's urging later in life, Annabelle said that her initial thought was outright rejection but on reflection she changed her mind. She remembered that she was one of those people who frequently said "they" should do something, "they" being that vague group of people in charge. Once she realised that she was being offered the opportunity to becoming one of "they", she changed her mind. She came to see a role in public life as obligatory. "This is my duty', she said on one occasion.[17]

Invariably well and appropriately dressed, the next consideration was what she would wear to the candidate interview. She was still in uniform and suitable civilian attire was unobtainable. As she told the ABC interviewer, "I had been in uniform for years and we had very few coupons (clothes like petrol and some foodstuffs were subject to tight rationing with the only currency to acquire such items being by using the strictly limited number of coupons issued under wartime regulation) and I seemed to have no clothes that were suitable".[18]

The QPP Executive in its role as agent for the Liberal Party called a meeting for the evening of 22 July 1946, a Monday, to interview and select two Senate candidates. They had interesting choices to make. Six candidates were to present themselves. Incumbent Senator Harry

Foll was expected to be one of the two, leaving five other candidates to compete for the remaining slot. There were a married woman and Annabelle, along with a Brisbane Roman Catholic solicitor, Neil O'Sullivan, and two others.

Annabelle claimed to have been "terrified" at the prospect of facing the selection panel. It was a claim she frequently made about her state of mind before being confronted by an unfamiliar audience, but on this occasion at least it was probably absolutely true. A far more experienced public speaker than Annabelle would have been daunted to stand against Foll, a Senator since 1917, a Gallipoli veteran, Minister and member of the War Cabinet. He was the sort of person like her father for whom she had great respect. She was also at a disadvantage against the other female candidate who had the perceived benefit of a husband. She had been tipped as 'a big chance' according to "QPP circles" in an article in the Brisbane afternoon newspaper, *The Telegraph*, but that and other favourable press coverage did not abate her nervousness about the outcome.[19]

Annabelle remembered that night in minute detail. Despite the positive press coverage about her prospects, she was convinced by people she spoke to that she would not be successful, later recalling:

> Anyway, I said my piece, and after a while I came home – I didn't wait until the end, I was so sure

> I wouldn't get it. I had a frightful headache, I remember. I came home, took my dog for a walk and went to bed. And the next thing I knew the telephone was ringing and I was being wakened up and asked if I would go in and be photographed by the *Courier-Mail*, as I had won the endorsement.[20]

Another person who did not expect her to win despite the press reports was political professional Charles Porter who was present on the night. He also disregarded her father's influence. In his view she had no party background.

Despite the nerves, Rankin obviously confounded her doubters. Porter later told the ABC:

> She made a splendid impression. She was a strikingly handsome young woman, with a fine lot of auburn hair and she had this ringing clear voice and she enunciated the principles that she believed in with such a fervour and dedication that was almost a passion that she quite moved the people, and the result was that Annabelle secured the position in the Senate that she held from that point on.[21]

The photograph in the *Courier-Mail* the next morning shows that she did manage to locate suitable clothing for the occasion. She is pictured wearing a dark jacket over a white blouse topped off by a small but jaunty hat worn at an angle, clearly not of army issue. The newspaper's report focussed on the demise of Senator Foll as well as on Annabelle's victory. The end of Foll's political career was "the sensation of the ballot" according to the *Courier-Mail* and the passed-over candidate was not happy about it. His ire was directed at the other successful candidate, Neil O'Sullivan, rather than Annabelle. He dropped hints to the press that his defeat had been due to certain unnamed "religious influences". In fact, Foll contributed to his own defeat because he had spent much of the time he was a Senator living in Sydney, an unforgivable sin in the eyes of Queenslanders. The other QPP Senator did not contest the ballot. Both he and Foll had been in the Senate since 1917 and they had fallen out in recent years which would also have contributed to the feeling it was time for change.

The QPP itself was in no doubt that the selection of Annabelle was the main story. Its August news bulletin to members praised the selection of Annabelle as:

> a triumph for the fighting qualities of the women members of the Party, who, week in and week out, have pressed their claim for greater representation in the affairs of the nation by women. Politically, Miss Rankin, is a 'find' and the Executive Member who persuaded her to submit a nomination is particularly happy with her selection.[22]

Diplomatically, the news bulletin avoided mentioning that the anonymous Executive Member was the male Charles Wanstall. The "fighting qualities" of the Women's Section of the QPP might also have contributed to his choice not to reveal his identity at the time.

In addition to the women's section of the QPP there was a separate organisation pressing for greater involvement for women, the Queensland Women's Electoral League. This organisation had championed the election of Irene Longan for one term to the State Legislative Assembly in the 1930s but Annabelle was not associated with it in anyway. In fact, her lack of association with any part of Queensland's fractious non-Labor side of politics was an advantage. Her father's role as an MLA and a Minister long before provided her with an acceptable pedigree without the taint of more recent allegiance.

Future events would prove that Wanstall and the other members of the QPP had every reason to be happy with the selection of both Rankin and O'Sullivan. The Executive committee showed considerable foresight with both their picks proving their worth. In 1949 the QPP formally merged with the Liberal Party of Australia and Annabelle became one of the Vice-Presidents of the Queensland Branch of the Liberal Party in 1950. In the Senate, O'Sullivan became Leader of the Government following the 1949 election. Annabelle joined him as Government Whip following the 1951 poll.

In the context of 1946, the QPP Executive's decision was a bold and insightful step into the future. Although the war was over and in general terms the future outlook was better than for any time since the late 1930s, the political prospects for the QPP were grim. Labor stayed in government in Queensland until 1957. Federally the future was equally bleak with the competent and popular Treasurer Ben Chifley taking over the prime ministership seamlessly following the death-in-office of wartime leader John Curtin in 1945.

Was it desperation that drove the QPP Executive to select the untried pairing of an unmarried woman, albeit one who had been in the services, and a Catholic solicitor? No, it was a vote of confidence in the future and, in particular, in a relatively young woman who had made a very good impression with her clear speaking voice and the conviction with which she expressed her views as well as her attractive appearance and pleasing manner.

A quarter of a century later, the Queensland Liberal Party pre-selection committee, the direct descendant of the former QPP Executive, chose Australia's first Aboriginal politician, Neville Bonner, to fill the casual Senate vacancy created by Annabelle's resignation in 1971.

Queensland Liberals could be ahead of their times.

The campaign trail in 1946

"Miss Rankin Won Hearts of Audience", a *Maryborough Chronicle* headline told its readers on 25 July 1946 in a report on a meeting in the town's Memorial Hall the previous evening, just two days after the Senate selection ballot in Brisbane.

"In a speech which lasted only eight minutes", the article under the headline began, "Miss Annabelle Rankin, one of the joint Liberal Country Party Senate team, and Queensland's first woman Senate candidate, made her first public appeal and at the same time fired the first shot in this year's Senate campaign." After listing the Queensland People's Party dignitaries present, the article continued, "The attendance of one hundred and fifty persons was one of the largest to attend a political meeting in Maryborough for years. A striking feature of the attendance was the predominance of women, who outnumbered men by almost two to one." The article went on:

> Miss Rankin must have been highly gratified with the response to her first public appearance in support of her candidature. Her short address was frequently interrupted by prolonged bursts of handclapping, led almost invariably by women in the audience. She was given a most attentive hearing.
>
> A well-modulated voice, good pronunciation and enunciation, ability to make her points clearly, concisely, and with good emphasis where needed, made it hard to believe that Miss Rankin was making her 'debut' to the public in the political sphere.
>
> 'This is one of the most thrilling moments in my

life,' said Miss Rankin. 'It is not just coincidence that I am in Maryborough tonight either. I wanted to come to Maryborough and I asked to do so because I belong here.

'I felt that I had to start out on this adventure into a strange new sphere in the place where so much of my life was spent and among the many good friends I have retained here since my departure' (applause).

'I am very pleased that the Party has placed such a responsibility on me. I want to tell my own townspeople first how I feel about this job I have undertaken.

'I offered my services because I honestly believe that the need of a woman's voice in the Senate is vitally necessary (applause). For a number of years I have worked with women's and children's organisations all over Queensland. I have been honoured and privileged to meet and know so many women and men of our fighting services during my service during the war years.

'I worked for those women and men during the war, and I want to go on working to help the woman and the wife during the years of peace (applause)

'Much has been said about the rehabilitation of men, but not so much has been said about the rehabilitation of women out of the services. The discharged service woman has her problems just as well as the man, and I want to help her in those problems. If I am given the opportunity of helping women to sort out their problems, I will be happy (applause).

'I accepted the responsibility of electing to do this job because I don't know of any better work in which I could be engaged, and because I have the time now to devote to it.

'I feel particularly for the young married woman with young children. I saw what they had to contend with during the war – the endless queues, the myriad difficulties which beset her path, and most of all, the loss of her partner. Now, in peace those heroic women are entitled to everything the nation can give them, and I want to help see that they get it(applause).

'I have the greatest admiration for Dame Enid Lyons and Senator Dorothy Tangney. Both prove conclusively the worth of women representatives in our Parliaments.

'Social legislation affects our women more closely than any other section of the community, and I believe that a woman's voice should be heard in all measures of social legislation aimed at improving the lot of our people generally.

'Happy homes, in my opinion, are the best foundation on which to attempt to build national progress, and I want to help to that most desirable end.'

The *Maryborough Chronicle* article concluded, "Resounding and prolonged applause marked the termination of Miss Rankin's address".[23]

Despite Liberal Party organiser Charles Porter's insistence that the campaigning in 1946 was enthusiastic but amateur, Annabelle's campaign got off to an excellent start on familiar ground in Maryborough. It was good staff work to get her there so quickly to capitalise on her recent selection. The strong interest shown by women voters in Maryborough which indeed must have gratified Annabelle was to be repeated throughout the state in the following weeks.[24]

Name recognition is vital for all political candidates and within a month the instantly recognisable phrase "Our Annabelle" was common currency in Queensland. In just over a month after her selection, the following headline appeared in the *Courier-Mail* on 28 August: *Marriage Can Wait, Says 'Our Annabelle'*.

The headline was over a report of a 250-strong meeting of a QPP Women's Advisory Committee lunch addressed by Annabelle and chaired by Liberal candidate for the seat of Brisbane, Geoff Ward. In the course of introducing her, Ward was quoted as saying, "We don't call her 'Miss Rankin' in the Party any more – she's 'our Annabelle' whether she likes it or not." Miss Rankin's retort was quoted as, "She likes it". [25]

With its cosy familiarity she happily adopted both the phrase "Our Annabelle" and her three-syllable Christian name to her advantage throughout her public life. In the Senate she was universally known simply as Annabelle by political friend and foe alike. Similarly, her personal signature was invariably boldly and clearly written as "Annabelle J. Rankin" be she addressing governors-general, prime ministers or constituents.

On the day after the QPP Women's Advisory Council function, Annabelle and O'Sullivan left for a six-day, 2,500 mile tour of northern and north western Queensland including Mackay, Charters Towers, Cairns, Atherton and Townsville. After the euphoria of the first Maryborough meeting this was the grind of election campaigning and Annabelle found it challenging. She commented later to the ABC about this campaigning:

> Oh dear, we were like a circus, you know, one-night stands. We would talk in one place and move on and talk again and, of course, accommodation wasn't nearly as good as it is now. It was just the end of the war. Our rail services had had a battering.

In the same interview, she remembered her dread at anticipating hostile and difficult questions from the floor following the formal speeches at the start of a meeting. "I was scared, always; and I was scared of waiting for that terrible moment of question time when wondering what you were going to be asked and if you would know the answer. And the chairman would look anxiously around and say 'Any questions? Isn't anybody going to ask a question?' And I used to think,' I hope not, I hope not'. And sometimes they did and sometimes they didn't."[26]

Annabelle tried the tactic of anticipating the inevitable questions about her single status by pre-emption. She raised the fact that she had faced criticism for not being married, and then provided the answer herself, "Many people think it is a pity I'm not married. If I were, I would not have time to stand for Parliament. They say it is a pity I have not had the experience of bringing up a family. Well, there is still time for that."[27]

At a time when the prevailing view was that a woman's place was in the home, and preferably in the kitchen, Annabelle was inevitably going to face hostility for being single from women as well as men. On one occasion at a meeting in a bush town, she handled questioning about her lack of children so adroitly that it attracted the attention of the interstate media, a Melbourne reporter noting:

> At a campaign meeting this week Miss Rankin was asked what she knew about the troubles and trials of country womenfolk, and she explained at length that she was country born and bred and knew all about them – the toil, the difficulties of educating children, the scarcity of medical facilities.

'Oh yes, but have you ever had a baby in the country?' asked a well-meaning lady. Miss Rankin crimsoned to the roots of her auburn hair and came back: 'No, I haven't.' Then added as an afterthought, 'Nor anywhere else'.[28]

Her Queensland federal parliamentary colleague Jim Killen shared many platforms with Annabelle and had a fund of anecdotes about the perils of outdoor meetings especially on the backs of trucks which was a common practice. Annabelle was very conscious of the need to maintain her poise which could be difficult for a person dressed in a skirt or a dress, as she invariably was, while clambering or being hoisted onto the back of a vehicle. To cope with this she took a portable step ladder whenever she was likely to encounter truck-back venues, both to save herself embarrassment and ensure she could approach the microphone or podium with composure.

One of Killen's often-told stories involved Annabelle's deft handling of a questioner who asked about her father, clearly not aware that he was already dead. As gently as possible she told the man that her father had passed away some years before but smoothed over the potentially difficult moment by adding, "... but I always feel that he is with us still'.[29]

Annabelle attracted considerable media attention because of her novelty value. As a Queensland first she was news. A side effect of this was that she overshadowed her Liberal running-mate on the Senate ticket, Neil O'Sullivan, although he was to be listed second on the joint Senate ballot with the Country Party while she was third. She received more attention both in public and in the media coverage. In articles on the meetings they both addressed, Annabelle received top billing and more column inches. There is no evidence O'Sullivan resented this treatment and it did not adversely affect their future relationship working together in the Senate initially in the small Opposition team and later in government.[30]

Her presentation on the platform clearly impressed her political colleagues and the journalists who covered her events but her contemporary speaking notes show that what she said, as opposed to how she said it, was not as impressive. There is a thick sheaf of papers in her Archives collection which, when compared with press articles on campaign events, are obviously her speaking notes for the 1946 campaign. The typing is in capitals, certain words and phrases are heavily underlined in red crayon for emphasis and annotations in her handwriting appear on several pages.[31]

These early papers reveal a clumsiness in her writing style, a lack of erudition. She was well, but not highly educated. Her forte was her instincts for her community, and she was quick to learn. The messaging outlined in an albeit badly constructed "stump" speech reveals a natural ability to tap into the issues of the moment. In 1946, her foremost theme was:

> The women of Australia have earned the right to share in the building of this brave new world because of their wonderful contribution to the war, during those years they did a magnificent job both on the home front and in the services, and as they gave much then, their voices must be heard in the peace time planning, and they must not be silent in the first years of the life of the new world.

Her message was resonating. Women were coming out in unprecedented numbers to see and listen to her. They responded well to her message so she and her political minders could reasonably expect that it would work at the ballot box as well. There was the added advantage that Annabelle passionately believed in what she was saying on women's representation, and this contributed positively to the conviction which was apparent and often commented on when she spoke in public.

Equally perceptive was her early focus on housing. Five pages of these early 1946 speech notes are devoted to "Housing" and conclude with, "The Liberal Party faces up to this need, and if elected will plan to enlarge the home building of the commonwealth, will ease restrictions and will speed up production of the necessary building materials. It fully realises that the future of this country is largely dependent on the solution of the housing problem".[32]

Although she expresses herself differently, Annabelle's beliefs and views about the centrality of home and family mesh with those of Robert Menzies as expressed in his *Forgotten People* speech in 1942 which in due course found their way into Liberal Party policies and Government priorities. It is impossible to know whether this was a happy coincidence, if Annabelle was drawing on election material supplied to her by Charles Porter or if she had heard and absorbed the ideas from hearing Menzies' broadcasts.

But, both as a candidate and later as a Senator, housing was an issue she returned to repeatedly. She focussed on the post-war housing camps near Brisbane where many families were forced to live due to the shortage of housing and young married couples having to spend years living with their parents. For her to later become Minister for Housing was an appropriate culmination of her political career.

Unsurprisingly another section of her speech notes was "Rehabilitation of the Ex-service Woman" . This issue was regularly included in her speeches with four pages devoted to the topic in the 1946 election speech notes. Annabelle had spent the previous three years of her life devoted to the welfare of service women. She had had plenty of time to think about the issues involved and had had to speak in public about them, as was the case in the talk she gave which so impressed Charles Wanstall and led to her becoming a Senate candidate.

It is apparent from the clarity and conciseness of the following statement that she knew what she was talking about and confident in how she expressed herself on issues affecting service women:

> It must be remembered that these girls gave up the best years of their lives to answer their country's need. They not only gave up the comfort of their homes and the security of their family life but they gave up the years in which they could have trained for a career, or in which they might have married.[33]

The second last section of her notes, "Are you Regimented", was only two pages long and the most overtly political section. With war time restrictions mostly still in place, opposition parties would naturally criticise the government in power for needless regulation. For the Liberal Party which believed in freedom for the individual it was also an ideological point of difference with Labor. Annabelle provided a female twist pointing out that red tape had negative consequences for housewives, business women and families.

The four page "Ending" section mainly reprised the "Beginning". The first paragraph was an exhortation, "So again I stress *men and* women of Queensland, you must be alive to your responsibilities and see that after the election in September, a woman's voice is heard in Canberra".[34] The words in italics – "men and" – were inserted in pencil. Annabelle had the conflict that all women candidates have about where their priorities lie. Are they are representing women only or the entire community? For Annabelle who was thrown in at the deep end with little background in her new role and little time to prepare, it is not surprising she would waver on this point.

After hectic weeks of campaigning in late July, August and up until polling day on 28 September, there was a long wait while the votes were counted. Although Labor knew it could be in trouble in the Queensland Senate contest from early in October, the official result confirming that Annabelle had been elected was not announced until several weeks later.

When the vote was announced and Annabelle declared elected, all her hard work was justified. Although she was third on the ticket she had attracted almost twice as many first preference votes as O'Sullivan who was above her on the ballot. Annabelle won 17,565 first preferences compared to O'Sullivan's 9,119. The detailed voting calculations showed that Annabelle had also attracted a considerable number of Labor preferences.

While the Queensland Senate outcome was pleasing for the new Liberal Party, there was little else to be pleased about. The result nationally was disastrous for the fledgling party and a severe blow to its leader Robert Menzies. The three Queensland Senators would sit among 33 Labor Senators. It was the last Senate election under block voting which gave a disproportionate number of seats to the winning party. The voting system was changed to proportional representation in 1948.

The outcome was equally disappointing in the House of Representatives. The Labor Government lost six seats in the lower house, two of which were to Independents. This left the Chifley Government with a comfortable majority of 43 seats, the new Liberal Party a sparse 17 and the Country Party 12. The overall 1946 outcome was a decisive ALP victory.

For Annabelle her stop-start existence would last for another year. The vagaries of the Australian electoral system meant that although her position as a Senator-elect was announced in October 1946, her six-year term as a Senator did not begin until July 1947. Then there was another delay because she was not sworn in as a Senator until Parliament met in October 1947.

A distraction took place in August 1947 when she was sent to Sydney to speak at a Liberal Party Rally against the Chifley Government's bank nationalisation plans. She was the only woman speaker but as the photograph which appeared in the *Sydney Morning Herald* the next day shows, nearly half those attending were women.

She was to discover that all interstate press were not as kindly disposed to her as the media outlets in her home state. In Sydney's the *Daily Telegraph* the next day a columnist wrote that Annabelle "made a great hit" when addressing the well-attended meeting but, "Oh boy, how she churns out the cliches!" The item went on to list them as "we must stand shoulder to shoulder", "we must put our shoulder to the wheel" "we are at the crossroads" and a few more, along with the pointed comment:

> There's no doubt about the matey-ness of Queenslanders. Senator Rankin said she's known in Queensland as 'our Annabelle' and wants people down here to think of her as their Annabelle, too. Shades of 'Call me Artie'.[35]

The weekly magazine *The Bulletin* rushed to her defence with a poem on another part of her address. "People regard me as an oddity, and expect me to look queer and to have no interest in hats, clothes or make-up, and no ability for ordinary household tasks. As a matter of fact, I'm proud of my cooking", she had said. The poet proclaimed:

> *How different the picture here projected*
> *From that which careless fancy often draws*
> *Of ladies whom constituents have selected*
> *To aid their fellow-men in making laws.*
> *Merely because she's managed an intrusion*
> *Into the ring where politicians mill,*
> *How utterly fantastic the illusion*
> *She's not a woman still!*[36]

Annabelle's performance in Sydney and the publicity it attracted bolstered her standing at home. At a meeting of QPP state parliamentary members press cuttings from her visit were circulated and discussed. One of their number, Ken Morris MLA, was deputised to, as his letter to her said, "convey to you their really sincere congratulations on your efforts – in Sydney and elsewhere. I am most happy to do so, and would like you to know we are all very proud of 'Our Annabelle'."[37]

Into parliament

In a cameo of Annabelle's political life, the author and historian Margaret Fitzherbert, wrote:

> When she was first elected to the Senate, Annabelle was aged in her thirties, unmarried and without children. Her image was far removed from that of the comforting mother represented by Dame Enid Lyons, and she did not need the name or reputation of a male relative to auspice her election to parliament...Annabelle Rankin was the first of a new generation of Liberal women who, with the support of the newly-unified liberal forces, entered the federal parliament after the war and dominated its female representation for years. After her death in 1986, Prime Minister Bob Hawke described Dame Annabelle in Parliament as 'a pioneer in the involvement of women in Australian federal politics and public life'.[38]

Canberra when Annabelle arrived in 1947 was more like country town Maryborough than bustling wartime Brisbane alive with men and women in Australian and United States uniforms. Parliament House where she worked and the Kurrajong Hotel where she lived were walking distance apart. The only other buildings in the immediate vicinity of Parliament House were a scattering of administrative blocks.

Was she to stand outside the double doors at the front of the then Parliament House, to her right was the walk to the Kurrajong and straight ahead in the distance directly to the north was the Australian War Memorial on the other side of the Molonglo River (now Lake Burley Griffin) at the foot of Mt Ainslie. Within walking distance to her left were the Hotel Canberra and Albert Hall. Not visible and barely worth visiting was the civic centre on the far side of the Molonglo.

The Kurrajong was not a commercial hotel but a government hostel mainly for members of Parliament. There were many other similar hostels around Canberra to house public servants and workers arriving in the expanding capital. Jim Killen was also a long-term resident of the Kurrajong. He did not arrive in Canberra until 1955 but his description holds true for when Annabelle arrived as the place changed little in the post war years:

> In those days members of Parliament stayed either

at the Canberra Hotel or at the Kurrajong. The Canberra Hotel was, in general terms, 'the home' of those Senators and members who commanded a measure of opulence ... The manageress of the Kurrajong Hotel was a most extraordinary woman – Gladys Cole. She was a large lady, with an extremely ample bosom. She had a firm, dominating character and gave the splendid impression of one of Her Majesty's battleships sailing into an Atlantic gale. She ran 'The Kurra' with great understanding of the frailties, strengths and hopes of the essentially political community that were her guests. 'The Kurra' was run on rather austere lines. Rooms were not heated. That drew from Artie Fadden the observation, 'When you get into bed on a winter's night the sheets crackle like a Sao biscuit.' Neither did the rooms have bathrooms or telephones.[39]

All new parliamentarians shared the same experiences of arriving in Canberra and becoming accustomed to their working and living environment. For Annabelle that was where the similarities stopped. As a young woman in an Opposition of only three in an unbalanced Senate she attracted far more attention than would otherwise have been the case had she been an incoming male backbencher from a safe and uninteresting electorate.

Annabelle was also immediately thrown into a prominent role outside Parliament due to the bank nationalisation issue which grew into the major point of difference between government and opposition parties through to the 1949 election. In addition, she was the butt of a joke by a former prime minister, pleasantly surprised by the gallantry of the serving prime minister and earned the approval of a future prime minister all within a short time of arriving in the national capital.

An essential part of the political rather than the parliamentary week is the party meeting at which the leader of the party whether prime minister or leader of the opposition presides. For backbenchers, particularly those from the Senate, it is one of the few occasions when they are in close proximity to their leader. Upcoming legislation is discussed but, often more important, are the politically sensitive matters which need to be raised and discussed in private. The Opposition party room after the 1946 election contained many important figures from the past, none more so than William Morris 'Billy' Hughes.

In her early days the essentially shy Annabelle sat at the back of the party room on a padded bench. On a memorably hot day she removed her new and rather smart hat placing it on the bench beside her. Entering the room late, as he always did, Billy Hughes spotted a spare seat and sat both on it and Annabelle's hat. Hughes turned on his ever-present hearing aid and settled down to listen to proceedings. As she told her biographer:

> I saw the edge of the brim protruding from beneath
> Mr Hughes. So, very quietly and slowly, I put my

hand down and worked towards the edge of it wondering if I could manage to pull it out from under him. As I was doing this, in this terrible silence, his voice rang out, as only his could, 'If you want to pick my pockets Annabelle do it quickly and don't fumble'. Everyone roared with laughter as I then retrieved my hat.[40]

Her next prime ministerial contact was with Joseph Benedict "Ben" Chifley. She found him to be quiet, unassuming and with an addiction to detective novels to relieve the stress of high office, a habit he passed on to her. Annabelle's earliest recollection of him occurred late on a Friday night when they met on the steps of Parliament House on their way back to "The Kurra" where they both stayed although Chifley had a larger room as befitting his status. She recalled him saying to her, " 'Are you walking down?' She said that she was. Then he said, 'I am walking down too and it is far too dark for you to walk alone. We will go together'." [41]

Annabelle did not discover until many years later that she had impressed a future prime minister, Robert Gordon "Bob" Menzies during her first term in the Senate. This fact came to light when she was appointed Minister for Housing 20 years later. A Canberra newsletter noted: "Sir Robert is believed to have remembered with affection her performance in the Senate between 1946 and 1949 when with Sir Walter Cooper and Sir Neil O'Sullivan she was one of only three members of Sir Robert's then

Opposition in the Senate".[42]

Those first years in the Senate were busier than Annabelle could have imagined. With only three Senators to fill the roles of an Opposition, Annabelle became the Opposition Whip. In addition to her parliamentary duties and political work outside the Senate, the Brisbane *Courier-Mail* engaged her to write a weekly column to appear every Monday. Her presence had also attracted the interest of the interstate press.

Reporting on the Senate's 1947 intake under the headline "Beauty and Wisdom in Senate", the Melbourne *Age* told its readers, "Eleven well-dressed men and a titian beauty, elected to the Senate more than a year ago, attended that dignified chamber today for the first time and took the oath of allegiance to the King". Later in the article a paragraph in bold type read, "The new woman member is Annabelle Jane Mary Rankin, formerly state secretary of the Girl Guides Association. She looked younger than her 38 years, and slightly nervous. Her cocoa-brown tailored frock blended nicely with a rich head of titian hair".[43]

The Melbourne *Age* article encapsulated the way in which Annabelle's arrival on the national political stage was reported. She was treated differently from her male colleagues because that was the way women were portrayed in the media in Australia at the time. Women's appearance and how they were dressed were then staples of journalism, hence the repeated references to the colour of her hair and her "frock". The extent of the coverage she received was due to a more timeless rule of journalism: "dog bites man" is not news but "man bites dog" is news. According to that rule, "man becomes politician" was less newsworthy in 1947 than "woman becomes politician".

Annabelle accepted the norms of the society she lived in and never publicly commented on the coverage she attracted. She did, however, carefully monitor everything written about her and kept all the articles and column items in meticulously maintained and curated clippings scrapbooks, one for each year. Compared with women politicians of later decades, Annabelle and her contemporaries did not have much to complain about. The somewhat condescending faux gallantry of the treatment of the woman parliamentary pioneers was less offensive than the overt sexism later female politicians had to endure.

There can be no doubt that the mostly favourable publicity Annabelle enjoyed had a positive impact on her political career. She was only accorded the first position on the joint Liberal-Country Party ticket at the last election she contested but from her position lower down the ticket she regularly attracted a personal vote of more than 15,000 first preferences, a high number for the then population of Queensland and more than any other candidate. This can be attributed in part to the media attention she received and generated herself whether about her political role, her hats, her clothes or her red, auburn and sometimes titian hair.

The first two of her Monday *Courier-Mail* columns provided a running commentary on her first weeks in the Senate. The Queenslanders who turned to page 7 of their local paper on 20 October in 1947 would have been puzzled to read the headline, "The Three Bears Will Growl Soon", over the by-line, "From Senator Annabelle Rankin". She was referring to the way one Labor Senator described Annabelle and her two Opposition colleagues who were effectively crowded out by the 33 Government Senators.

Annabelle responded stoutly, "So far we have not begun to growl, but although our numbers are small, we will yet be heard in no uncertain manner". Her final paragraph was less assertive and exhibited a measure of the nervousness the Melbourne *Age* reporter noticed, "I have not yet spoken in the Senate. I do so in a few days' time, but I feel sure the atmosphere is not easy to speak in because there is so much movement".[44]

Speaking in parliament is different from speaking at a meeting to which she was already accustomed. At a public meeting the audience is seated and usually listens attentively to the speakers. In the parliamentary forum the politicians often chat among themselves paying no attention to the person actually speaking. There is constant movement in the chamber as attendants walk in and out delivering messages, the Hansard writers come and go as they start and finish their period of taking down the proceedings in shorthand and other Senators stroll in and out of the chamber at will. This was the atmosphere which was worrying Annabelle who was due to deliver her maiden speech two days later on Wednesday 22 October.

More than just a bustling Senate chamber was to distract Annabelle in the week ahead. The *Courier-Mail* presented her Monday column more distinctly this time with its own heading "My Week in Parliament" accompanied by a head and shoulders photograph. Her column began rather prosaically, "Women have been news this week" and went on:

> You've read that 1,000s came to Canberra to protest against the nationalisation of banking, and to demand a referendum. At their meeting in the Albert Hall, near Parliament House, I seconded the resolution moved by Dame Enid Lyons MHR, and spoke with her against the proposed legislation. We both had to leave early – she to speak in the House of Representatives, and I to make my maiden speech in the Senate.[45]

The less-than-ideal preparation for her maiden speech did not adversely affect Annabelle's presentation. A weekend newspaper offered no hint of the nervousness or other sign of discomfort reported previously, observing, "Senator Rankin's flawless enunciation and her carefully chosen words gave a repertory theatre flavour to her speech".[46] On this occasion her words were indeed carefully chosen. The whole speech which took 20 minutes to deliver, was free of cliches and bore all the hallmarks of thorough preparation. She began:

> I rise to make my initial speech in this chamber with a feeling blended of pride and humility – pride, because of the honour of Senatorship that has been conferred on me by the people of Queensland, my native State; and humility in the knowledge that every member of the National Parliament will need strength and divine guidance in the tasks that lie ahead of all of them.

After more of the same sentiments, Annabelle began growling: "It seems to me, a woman with no pretensions to being seer or prophet, that first things are being forgotten and progress arrested, while those in power indulge their passion for political and economic experiments that are highly dangerous". She went on to criticise the Chifley Government for insufficient attention to defence, a common theme among those parliamentarians who had served in the recent war. She then changed tack to define how she saw her role as a woman in the Senate, beginning by stating she did not see herself as representing only the women in her electorate:

> However, I believe that at times it will be necessary to assert the rights and express the viewpoint of those for whom there is no such thing as organised

unionism, no such thing as pressure politics or a 40-hour week – the home-makers, particularly those in the lonely places of Australia.[47]

This section of Annabelle's speech was singled out in the first comprehensive book on women in politics in Australia as encapsulating the ambivalent position of early women parliamentarians. As the authors saw it, "On one hand they could not afford to disturb the universe of existing social expectations. On the other, because of the vulnerability created by these social expectations, most of them acknowledged a special responsibility to defend in the public realm the interests of women and children".[48]

Continuing her maiden speech, Annabelle linked her intention to speak up for women in general to the other woman in the Senate:

> For that reason, I feel there is a strong womanly bond between myself and the honourable Senator from Western Australia, who has the distinction of being the first woman ever to become a member of the Senate. There are things that transcend party politics, and Senator Tangney may be sure that in anything designed to help the women of Australia, or the children who are in their care, she can count on my ready and sincere interest.[49]

That was the last concession to bipartisanship in her speech. The remainder, which constituted nearly three-quarters of its content, was devoted to a sustained and well-researched analysis of the Postmaster-General's Department and its Minister, Senator Cameron, Deputy Leader of the Government in the Senate. Annabelle started growling in earnest:

> I propose to direct this, my first speech in this august chamber, to an earnest appeal to the Postmaster-General for greater consideration and better services for the women of Australia...If they are to feel adequately protected against emergency, accident and sickness, then it will be because of the communication services provided by the Postmaster-General. Nothing has done more to alleviate the loneliness of the outback than the postal services. These services are so interwoven with the texture of the daily lives of our women that they are necessities, not luxuries. What a pity it is, then, that so little has been done to enlarge and develop the Postmaster-General's services in their application to the home, and to encourage their use by women to whom they mean so much. Obviously, it is not a question of money.[50]

Annabelle proceeded with a forensic analysis of the failings of the Post-Master General's Department and its Minister. Its latest report to Parliament was two years in arrears and the different divisions were making multi-million dollar profits while providing inadequate services. She revealed that the postal service made a profit of two and a half million pounds which plainly indicated unnecessarily high charges. Her solution was the introduction of a new class of mail, the family and social letter, to be carried at a reduced rate of a penny or a penny and a half.

Likewise, the telephone section was making a three million pound profit. Annabelle's suggestion was for reduced charges of ten shillings for installation and ten shillings for half a year's rental. The telegraph section was a similar story with a one million pound profit. Her recommendation was for consideration of a special rate for family and social telegrams of six pence per twelve words. Annabelle concluded in fine style wrapping up the specific content of her speech into both her own focus on women especially those living in isolation and her party's emerging themes of home and family:

> During the last few years, much has been said in this chamber about social services. May I remind honourable Senators that one of the great social services is the service rendered to the home by the Postmaster-General's Department; that this service reaches all homes, rich or poor, in one or more of its activities; and that this great department serves all classes, all creeds, and, in fact, all Australians?
>
> I ask for a new realisation of how much it can do for the housewife – a new orientation of the department's approach to its service, and a policy decision that this department must develop, expand, and cheapen its 'home and social' services to the lasting benefit of the women of Australia,

and to the upholding and uplifting of the ideal of the home as the basic unit of society.[51]

In her *Courier-Mail* column Annabelle wrote that she was delighted and encouraged to receive many letters and telegrams congratulating her on her maiden speech.

Annabelle was followed immediately by Senator O'Sullivan whose maiden speech marked a crescendo of growling. After brief opening pleasantries he expressed his disappointment at the tone and subject-matters of previous speakers on the Government side:

> To honourable Senators from whom I had hoped to learn something of the manner in which the Government proposed to use its majority in both houses to implement a policy of progress and development, I listened intently, but in vain ...The addresses of most ... honourable Senators were more in keeping with the hustings, the soap-box and the street corner, than the traditions of this chamber.[52]

In keeping with Annabelle's prediction, the new Opposition Senators were making themselves heard in no uncertain manner. A Government Senator of the same Irish heritage as O'Sullivan expressed his sorrow that such a speech could have been uttered by someone whose name began with an 'O' and an apostrophe.

For the remainder of 1947 and the first half of 1948, the Leader of the Opposition in the Senate, Senator Cooper of the Country Party, undertook most of the speaking duties in the chamber. This was because of his greater experience and the inevitable consequence of being Leader. The situation changed in the second half of 1948 when Senator Cooper was overseas as a member of a parliamentary delegation.

The dramatic increase in Annabelle's speaking workload can be gauged from the Index of Speeches at the end of each session's Hansard. Where Annabelle's speeches and questions took up less than a column initially, her listing in the second half of 1948 extended over three columns. Senator O'Sullivan's entries over the same period covered five columns as he was acting Leader of the Opposition as well.

The record of divisions in the Senate which show how each Senator votes was even more lopsided for the latter half of 1948. The Hansard faithfully shows Annabelle as "Teller" for the Opposition as befitting her role as Opposition Whip, though it was not a difficult task to count her own vote and then that of Senator O'Sullivan.

Although her task of fulfilling half the work of an entire opposition was onerous, it was also immensely rewarding. In only her second year in parliament she had the opportunity to be directly involved and speak on the full range of government activity. From Aborigines and the Australian Broadcasting Commission through the alphabet to War Graves and Waterfront, she had unrivalled experience of handling the complexities of parliamentary debate and proceedings.

She also kept a close eye on her maiden speech topic of the Postmaster-General's Department especially on finding in its 1946 annual report that the Brisbane GPO was not included in plans to modernise the chief telegraph offices in most capital cities.

Annabelle pursued the issue and Postmaster-General Senator Cameron soon had good news. Brisbane's needs had been reconsidered since preparation of the annual report and a new post office was to be built. "Indeed", the Postmaster-General concluded, "I shall derive as much satisfaction as the honourable Senator in seeing the work commenced as early as possible".[53]

Senator Cameron seemed to be enjoying his exchanges with Annabelle. He took the opportunity to provide an update on the Brisbane GPO work during the Budget debate. A total of 600,000 pounds was to be spent on the first section, with the Minister commenting, "That should be most satisfactory to members of the Opposition, and I trust that I shall be privileged to open the new building in their presence".[54]

Annabelle was still not satisfied and asked him when the new building was to start. Cameron replied that preliminary work had begun which caused O'Sullivan to interject, "Will the Postmaster-General get on with the work before the Government goes out of office at the end of next year?" Unphased Senator Cameron retorted:

> I believe that I shall be Postmaster-General long enough to officiate at the opening of the new Brisbane Post Office and that I shall have the pleasure of extending an invitation to the Honourable Senator to the opening ceremony.[55]

Another matter of concern to her female constituency was the acute shortage of white cotton thread. She drew attention to the problem in a question to the government and followed up with another when it was clear the government's efforts to rectify the lack of supply were failing. This line of questioning on shortages of household goods such as cotton and matches fed into the larger narrative of Labor Government regulations causing unnecessary hardship.

Following issues of interest to the people they represent by asking questions and probing during debates is normal fare for parliamentarians in opposition. But the sustained attention to detail and level of activity required by Annabelle and Senator O'Sullivan was abnormal. In one evening of detailed consideration of the Budget, the two Queenslanders were repeatedly on their feet rising to speak on a dozen different items of expenditure in less than an hour.

Annabelle was first questioning the seemingly high cost of sending an Australian delegation overseas to the International Labour Organisation (ILO). Senator O'Sullivan wanted to know why an apparently parsimonious amount of five hundred pounds was to be provided to the Boy Scout movement which did such good work. He had the satisfaction of drawing from the Minister responding an undertaking to take his urging for a greater amount back to Cabinet.

Annabelle questioned why there was no appropriation for development and experimental work on soya beans as had been the case in previous years and was told that this work had been taken over by the States. O'Sullivan was on familiar ground wanting to know why the Commonwealth had spent more than twenty-seven thousand pounds on legal fees and expenses associated with the controversial Banking Act stating that it was a shame the country was being put to that expense. The temporary presiding officer quickly shut down debate on this tricky issue for the government despite protests from O'Sullivan.

Then it was Annabelle's turn to be on familiar territory, spending by the Department of Social Services on a housekeeper service. She asked the responsible minister who was a Senator Nick McKenna for details, and they were forthcoming. Consideration turned to Commonwealth Railways and Annabelle suggested that trained hostesses should be on the trans-Australia trains to assist women and children on that long journey.

The Postmaster-General's Department was next and both Queenslanders participated. O'Sullivan wanted to know why the appropriation for the Australian Broadcasting Commission was increasing so much. He was told it was due to increased labour and cost of living costs. Annabelle probed at the amounts accounted for by technical services, where funds were coming from for educational programs and did they cover items such as concerts?

Before the sitting was over, expenditure on New Guinea, the Northern Territory and Norfolk Island had to be considered. Annabelle asked why the expenditure provided for Aboriginal affairs in the Northern Territory was so much lower than that for New Guinea but only received a vague response from the Minister. She was, however, pleased that five hundred pounds was to be spent on library services on Norfolk Island.[56]

With the return of Senator Cooper from overseas and resumption of his role as Leader of the Opposition in the Senate, Annabelle's parliamentary role in 1949 was far less challenging than during the latter half of the previous year. The Index for Senate speeches for the first session of 1949 tells the story. In the period of sittings from 9 February to 17 March Senator Cooper's entries cover two columns, Senator O'Sullivan's, half a column and Annabelle's, a third of a column.

Her speeches and questions were all aimed at probing government failings and unpopular actions with a view to the election towards the end of the year. Her longest and most detailed speech was on housing. This was an issue on which the government was vulnerable, which the Liberal Party had identified as a policy priority both post-war and beyond, and in which she had shown a consistent interest. As she said:

> We need a more comprehensive housing plan – a plan that will go right to the very root of the trouble and stimulate the production and distribution of building materials. The people of Australia know whom to blame for their troubles. They blame this Government because they have looked to it in vain for some relief from their desperate situation...They need homes, and it is the duty of the Government to ensure that they shall get homes.[57]

As outlined in her speech, Annabelle had direct evidence of the housing shortage because her frequent references to the issue in the media resulted in constituents writing to her outlining their problems:

> I draw attention of honourable Senators to the situation of two family groups in Queensland whose conditions were brought to my notice by letter. One writer stated:
>
> *'I live in a 12 by 14 tent with my husband and seven of my eight children. My children's ages are 16, 14, 13, 10, 8, 7 and 4, and I cook in a stove in a galley away from the tent. Life is very hard'.*
>
> It is deplorable that adolescent children should

have to live with their parents in one tent. Surely this is not our vaunted post-war standard of living in this post-war Australia! The other letter I received stated:

> 'We were living in a room 10 by 10 with veranda 9 by 6. There was my husband and boy and married daughter with her baby 18 months old. She had to sleep on a mattress on the floor with her baby. We were all in one room'. [58]

Most of her questions were similarly politically directed. When the Federal Government wrote to all dentists on an administrative matter, many of the recipients feared this was the first step towards nationalisation of their profession. When Annabelle raised this matter in the Senate, she was told that the dentists' concerns were false propaganda. She received more evasive answers when she questioned ministers about shortages of goods from rice to fencing wire.

The 1949 election campaign in November and December was of vital importance to the Opposition but less so to Annabelle herself. She was not up for election so the Liberal Party made good use of her speaking skills and press appeal. She supported candidates in Tasmania, Victoria, New South Wales and South Australia in the early weeks and back in Queensland in the later stages. Shortly before election day Annabelle told 75 women in Ipswich, west of Brisbane, that "Socialism is the issue – socialism or freedom". She was speaking in support of the Liberal candidate for the electorate of Oxley in which Ipswich was the main urban centre.[59]

Annabelle's efforts in Queensland, as well as those of many others, were amply rewarded. The Coalition's 27 seat majority in the House of Representatives was "substantially a Queensland defeat of Labor. We supplied half of Menzies' total majority", according to the Liberal Party Queensland agent Charles Porter. He could make that claim because Queensland returned 15 Coalition members of the lower house compared to only three for Labor, and Queensland and Tasmania were the only states to send more than twice as many Coalition as Labor representatives to Canberra. The bulk of Coalition members still came from New South Wales and Victoria with 20 MHRs apiece.[60]

The Senate outcome was less of a triumph for the new government with the Labor Party, now in opposition, still in majority. There was disappointment too for Annabelle who was pushed aside by the incoming Liberal tide. Liberal Senators chose Senator Reg Wright from Tasmania as Whip. It was not an unreasonable choice. Wright had been a member of the Tasmanian Parliament which would have counted in his favour. It was going to be a difficult period for the new Menzies Government in the Senate. The ALP would inevitably use its majority in the Senate to frustrate efforts to pass laws dealing with banking and the communist party where there were deep ideological and political divisions between the parties.

Disappointment

Annabelle's *Courier-Mail* column welcoming the new Menzies Government to Canberra masked her personal disappointment:

> It seems strange to be sitting on the Government side of the Senate chamber after the years of sitting in Opposition. It is grand and cheering to see our members – 24 at present – instead of just the three of us. I am thrilled at the strength of Queensland representation in the new Parliament...There were also, of course, the largest number of women ever in the Federal Parliament – four Senators and Dame Enid Lyons in the House of Representatives.[61]

Along with losing her position as Whip in the Senate, she saw the three ex-servicemen who were in the lower house but who were also elected in 1946, and with whom she identified, all advance while she went backwards. Former airman Bill Falkinder, Member for Franklin, and naval officer, John Howse, Member for Calare, were appointed as ministerial under-secretaries while Jo Gullett, Member for Henty and a former army officer, became Chief Government Whip in the House of Representatives.

Enid Lyons had become a Minister, the first women to do so, but without a department to administer, and Annabelle turned to her to commiserate. The two women knew each other well by this time. They appeared together at bank nationalisation protest meetings and conferred on child endowment. Dame Enid stayed with Annabelle in May 1949 when she visited Brisbane to be guest speaker at an Empire Day function.

Lyons later recalled, "I think she felt frustrated very often because on one occasion she came down to my room in Parliament House almost in tears – in fact I'm not sure that she did not shed tears, saying that she thought there was no hope for women to succeed to that extent because of the general attitude towards women". Dame Enid went on to offer the sage advice to Annabelle that she would be accepted, "So long as you manage to do the work that men do and do it as well, and at the same time don't antagonise them".[62]

Annabelle never spoke publicly about this setback but from the evidence of her actions in the year and a half between the Coalition victory at the end of 1949 and the double dissolution election in April of 1951 she metaphorically dried her tears and restored her political fortunes, adhering closely to Lyons' advice.

Speaking opportunities were fewer with the greater number of Senators. Annabelle made the most of the first available slot, the Address-in-Reply debate following the Governor-General's speech formally opening a new Parliament after an election. Gone was the focus on women and children. This 25 minute speech was themed around migration and national development. She began with a call for more fitting recognition of Australia Day with planning and observation being taken over by the Commonwealth. The rationale for this was to provide newly arrived migrants with some sense of pride, loyalty and allegiance to their new country. She said:

> By encouraging these new Australians to appreciate the Australian way of life and the part we are playing in the great British Empire we can build Australia Day into a day as significant to this country as is Independence Day to the United States of America.[63]

This led into the need for more and better English language training, particularly to help the newly arrived at work as well as socially. The point provided her with a chance to remind the Senate of the good work voluntary groups including the Young Women's Christian Association and the Girl Guides were doing for new settlers.

The creation of a new Department of National Development was referred to in the Governor-General's speech and Annabelle urged that priority be given to northern Australia for defence as well as development reasons. She emphasised a common theme, "The development of Northern Australia poses a problem that challenges this nation, because this vast country with its many natural resources is as poor in planning as it is rich in potentialities". She went on to speak glowingly of Queensland's existing and potential resource projects, especially Mt Isa, as well as the prospects for an expansion of beef production. She finished with a reminder that all these developments needed a master plan to co-ordinate the necessary population and transport that would be needed.[64]

It was as good a speech as those delivered by most male parliamentarians. Annabelle had been appointed Deputy Whip by her Liberal colleagues and she made the most of that position to demonstrate she could fulfil the required duties as well as any other Senator. Support for her came from an unexpected source.

After a few weeks of the new Parliament Opposition Senator Ben Courtice rose to criticise the government Whip, Senator Wright. He said Wright had not endeared himself to Senators since becoming Whip and compared him unfavourably to Senator Rankin when she was Whip. He claimed that Wright had "manoeuvred Annabelle" out of her former position in which "she had done her duties just as effectively, without any emolument, and with much more charm".[65]

Courtice may have been genuinely motivated by loyalty to Annabelle as a fellow Queenslander. He was a sugar farmer like her father. It is more likely that Wright had annoyed him in some way. Wright was a strange choice for a Whip whose main role is to ensure that the Senators of his party turn up to vote and vote according to the party line. His subsequent long term as a Senator is most memorable for the number of times he crossed the floor on matters of principle, legality, and parliamentary prerogative. Although a lawyer and an educated man Wright appeared rough-hewn. The press gallery joke about him was that Tasmania had given him a pair of boots and sent him to Canberra. In fact, he was an erudite and enlightened man, often quoting poetry in his speeches. Wright was a significant parliamentarian but could be an annoying colleague.

The situation facing the Menzies Government in the Senate would have challenged a more diplomatic and persuasive personality than Wright. The Government was in minority but needed to pass two pieces of legislation to meet election promises. They were measures to reverse Chifley's bank nationalisation and to ban the Communist Party. Labor was committed to opposing both measures but was wary of outright rejection of legislation which would trigger a double dissolution election which, on the evidence of the 1949 voting trend, they would be likely to lose. It was a cat and mouse game which lasted for more than a year.

After the 1949 election Senator Neil O'Sullivan became Leader of the Government in the Senate and, "...exhibited finesse, courtesy and a quiet and thorough legislative and procedural skill that facilitated the Government's business, as when in October (1950), in an unprecedented procedural drama, he engaged in a battle of tactics with the Opposition as it tried (unsuccessfully in the end) to prevent the Government calling on a simultaneous dissolution".[66]

Annabelle meanwhile put the time to good use as a member of the Joint Parliamentary Committee on Public Works. She was the first woman to sit on that statutory joint committee and focussed on improving amenities for women in government buildings. She also continued to carry out her duties in the non-official position of deputy government whip which included being Acting Whip during Wright's month-long absence towards the end of 1950.

There were some unexpected pleasant moments. In June 1950, Senate proceedings came to a halt to allow a Labor Senator to present Annabelle with a bouquet of roses. It was the Opposition's tribute for a fair, courageous and intelligent political foe.[67] Six months later in June 1951, following a double dissolution in March and a general election in April, she was elected Government Whip in her own right.

Whip in Government

The party Whip is a member of parliament who is chosen by their team to be the team manager. Whips have several responsibilities, including:

- meeting with the whips of opposing parties to plan the parliamentary day, set the agenda and sort out procedural details;
- organising a list of party members who wish to speak on bills and other business and giving this

to the President of the Senate or the Speaker of the House of Representatives;

- making sure that all party members attend and vote as a team in a division;
- counting and recording the votes in a division;
- providing advice and support for party members;
- ensuring that party decisions are carried out;
- negotiating 'pairs' from opposing parties, so that numbers between the government and opposition are kept in balance if members of parliament are absent.

The term Whip comes from the sport of fox-hunting in England. The whipper-in was the person who whipped all the hunting hounds into a pack, pointed them in the right direction to chase the fox and ensured that the pack did not stray.[68]

Annabelle's account of the origins of Whip is more romantic than the official description above. She preferred the version that, when faced with a vital vote in the House of Commons, the Prime Minister of the day summoned his henchmen and instructed them to, "Whip them from the hunting fields of England and the pleasant haunts of Paris" to get them back to Westminster to vote. "And so from that day onwards the term Whip became well-known and the official term. I can assure you that when I whipped I had nothing as exciting to contend with as the hunting fields of England or the pleasant haunts of Paris," she added.[69]

She did her whipping from a small suite of rooms designated M45 which from the outside looked like any other office in Parliament House. They were mostly tiny rooms which had to serve as offices for two and sometimes three backbenchers following the post-war expansion of Parliament. The Senate nearly doubled in size from 36 in the 1946 election to 60 in the 1949 poll. Some of the tiny offices were so far from the Senate and House of Representatives chambers that when the bells rang summoning them to vote, their occupants often had break into a run to reach the chambers before the doors were locked and they were excluded from the chamber and unable to record their vote.

M45 had neither of those shortcomings. It was of adequate, if not generous, size and could not have been closer to the Senate chamber. Through its door opening off the Government lobby were two offices, the first and smaller for a staffer and the second and larger for the Government Whip. Beyond the offices were two private corridors, one leading into the Senate chamber and the other running behind the President of the Senate's Chair to the office of the Opposition Whip. The second private corridor facilitated that vital part of the Whip's role to meet with their opposite number to plan the daily working of the upper house.

M45 was Annabelle's work space for an unbroken 15 years. In the Liberal Party lower house government whips are chosen by the Prime Minister but the Senate whips are selected by a vote of Liberal Senators. It was one of Annabelle's proudest boasts that she was chosen by the vote of her peers after each and every election from 1951 to 1963.

The Menzies Government's position in the Senate improved from being in minority to a majority of four following the 1951 double dissolution election. As a result, her task was easier than that which faced the ill-fated Senator Wright whose tenure lasted little more than a year between the 1949 election at the end of that year to the double dissolution poll in April 1951. She had the added advantage that her Queensland colleague Neil O'Sullivan was Leader of the Government in the Senate, and they were accustomed to working together.

Annabelle earned the respect of her colleagues as evidenced by her successive re-election but she was not universally liked on her own side. In the course of her work, she had to undertake unpopular tasks such as cancelling leave, summoning colleagues back to Canberra unexpectedly, telephoning at inconvenient hours and on weekends. Most accepted her interventions as part of the job but at least one harboured a festering grudge.

Nancy Buttfield who won her place in 1955 was the first woman elected to the Senate from South Australia. Her father had been one of founders of the Holden motor car company and the press gallery joke about her was that she had been born with a silver bumper bar in her mouth, a quip attributed to acid-mouthed South Australian MHR Clyde Cameron. Buttfield accused Annabelle of behaving like a head prefect. She may have been motivated by other considerations because, as detailed later, she was capable of being two-faced as well as bearing a grudge.[70]

A year after becoming Government Whip in June 1951 Annabelle was chosen to go with Labor Senator Don Willesee as a member of a parliamentary delegation to Canada. On the final day of sitting before her departure, Labor Whip Senator Jack Critchley, said, "I trust that the harmonious relations that have existed between Senator Annabelle Rankin and myself in the years we have served together in this Senate as party whips will not be broken on her return. If they should be broken, she will have a difficult job to repair them."[71]

Fortunately, harmonious relations remained intact, as they did subsequently with younger Opposition whips who succeeded Senator Critchley who was a First World War veteran and shared Annabelle's close interest in returned service issues. Later in life Annabelle maintained she had been good friends with all her opposite numbers although it seems unlikely that she experienced no friction with her political opponents for a decade and a half in an often highly-charged political atmosphere. She certainly had no personal disagreements with Tasmanian Senator Justin O'Byrne when he was Opposition Whip. Annabelle's reverence for those of her parliamentary colleagues who had been in the armed services has been noted, and this was particularly the case with O'Byrne who was a decorated air force flier and German prisoner-of-war who had managed to escape in one of the fabled breakouts.

Elgin Reid was the Brisbane *Courier-Mail's* press gallery correspondent for much of the 1950s. He kept in close contact with Annabelle and she frequently featured in his articles. His opinion was that Annabelle, a relatively young woman in a man's world, was able to exert authority over her male colleagues in part because most of them were her own age and because she too had been in the services like so many of them.

There were other factors. It is true there was an unusual bond across the political divide because so many post-war parliamentarians had the shared wartime experience. In addition, they were all thrown together in the then small town which was the embryonic national capital where there was little else to do but interact with fellow parliamentarians.

More than those external factors, Annabelle was appreciated by her peers for being a hard worker, a hard Whip and good at what she did. Testament to this comes from fellow Queensland Senator Ian Woods which has added credibility because Woods like Wright was independent-minded and on almost as many occasions voted against his Government, making her life difficult. In Woods' opinion Annabelle was "capable and had the capacity the same as men Senators. You see you don't have to be one of these strident women to be a successful woman. Dame Annabelle Rankin was a very successful Senator because she wanted everyone else to work. When she was Whip, she saw that you worked, and because of her quality and her work she rated the same as anybody else."[72]

Her counterpart from the House of Representatives, Hubert Opperman, observed that proportional representation invariably returned Senate members at crisis levels, adding to the already well-known pressures of a Whip's role:

> An irksome minority fortunately balanced by some equality on each side, were crankily and perversely entering the seventh age of man and, often a crucial vote could swing on an irresponsible duo preferring to debate in the bar. Before a vital division, Annabelle often patrolled the danger zone, personally turning back any problem child, or leaving her equally strong-minded secretary, Olive Ashcroft, to hurry them along as the bell rang.
>
> She lived in a perpetual state of anxiety from their (her Senate colleagues) inescapable vicissitudes

of such matters as ill health, missed and delayed aircraft, sudden decease, family problems, sheer undutiful neglect and, because of her widespread popularity in Queensland, the abnormal demands made for her appearances by the State headquarters.

Impelled by fierce loyalty to the Party and urged by an inherited sense of service discipline she was scathing in her reproof of delinquents who, as males, meekly accepted from her far more extreme censure than they would have taken from one of their own sex. As a female, she could never exhibit any sign of weakness to her varied charges, but in later years in my office as a colleague in arms, she often confided her difficulties and indulged in occasional tension-relieving tears. [73]

Annabelle had taken heed of Enid Lyons advice given at a low point in her career. She had set out to do the work that men did and do it as well as they did, as a Senator and as a Whip. Dame Enid also told her not to forget that her femininity was an asset but should not be used as a weapon. That was something that Annabelle did not need to be told.

After the half-Senate election in 1953 Annabelle was re-elected as Government Whip unopposed. *The* Brisbane *Telegraph* reported, "It was not gallantry that kept the other members of the Senate out of the ballot for whip last week, but simply the knowledge that they did not stand a chance against the efficient Senator Rankin". [74]

Before the year was over Annabelle's hold over her own side and relationship with her opposite number were put to the test. The Government majority in the Senate was very slim, down to one or two votes. In those circumstances disputes can quickly flare up over seemingly trivial matters. During a debate one evening late in September, Government Senators made disparaging references to the absence of the Leader of the Opposition in the Senate, Senator McKenna. The normally unflappable Opposition Whip, Senator Critchley, took offence and lost his temper. Heated words of an unparliamentary nature were exchanged.

When tempers had cooled down Annabelle explained that McKenna's absence was justified because he and the Leader of the Government in the Senate had been invited to dinner with the Governor-General. The two leaders had been "paired" which excused them from attendance in the chamber but there had not been time to inform other Senators that this had occurred. Senator Critchley accepted her explanation and settled the matter saying, "I very much regret the incident which occurred tonight. For the first time in a fairly long political career, that incident provoked in me something resembling heat. It was distinctly unfair and I hope that a similar occurrence will never again be witnessed in this chamber'.[75]

Tempers flared again on the last day of sitting but this time Annabelle could not remedy the situation. On this occasion the dispute was about one Senator allegedly deliberately misquoting another and refusing to withdraw the remark when called on to do so by the President. Following this refusal by Senator Don Willesee, the process to suspend him from the Senate was set in motion. Instead of allowing the suspension to proceed in the normal manner, the Labor Party called for a division, that is a vote on whether Senator Willesee should be suspended or not. Annabelle did not have sufficient warning. Three government Senators failed to turn up for the vote which was won by the Opposition with a majority of one vote. Senator Willesee stayed in the Senate, and the Labor Opposition enjoyed a rare victory. A few hours later all appeared to have been forgiven as Senators including the whips exchanged the traditional end of session good wishes. Senator Critchley said he appreciated the assistance he had received from Annabelle. During their time as opposing whips, "There has never been a semblance of ill-feeling and that every action of the Honourable Senator has been of the highest standard."[76]

Annabelle replied in kind, adding that, "when such a spirit of friendship and co-operation exists, the tasks that must be done are made much more simple". [77] Annabelle concluded by hoping that the new year would be a very good one for all Australians. It would indeed be so for her because it was to begin with one of the highlights of her career, the Royal Visit by the then new Queen Elizabeth. Thirty years later recalling those events of February 1954 both for her biography and an oral history interview she clearly remembered her excitement at the Opening of Parliament which took place a few feet in front of her in her chamber, the Australian Senate.

By contrast Annabelle never recalled in later life meeting and being singled out for particular attention by then US Vice President Richard Nixon also in Canberra less than a year previously. Nixon had congratulated the Australian Parliament on having a female Whip. Although Nixon went on to become President and a prominent global figure, for Annabelle as a traditionalist and dedicated monarchist there was no question of which event would dominate her memory. Describing the Queen's visit, she told her biographer:

> I shall never forget that exciting day when she opened parliament in the Senate chamber. It was marvellous to sit in the Senate and await her arrival...As we sat in our places awaiting her arrival it was for me as though quite suddenly all the most beautiful things of history had come to pass. [78]

Annabelle's recollections are not astray. A Menzies biographer recorded, "In terms of sheer splendour the Canberra visit, though it came in early in the piece, was undoubtedly the high point of the tour. The Queen opened parliament in her coronation robes and jewels, after entering Parliament House along the traditional red carpet[79]

Annabelle was very aware of what the Queen was wearing, noting, "Then, with her understanding of people and knowing how everyone would want to see her coronation robe, she came in on one side of the great long table and left on the other side so that both sides would be able to view this historic gown...".[80]

Photographs of the occasion show the Queen is seated in the Senate President's chair, the centre of everyone's attention. Annabelle, in a smart blue-grey outfit replete with her service medals, is seated in her usual place on the end of the row of seats directly behind the front bench. Once the members of the House of Representatives were seated in the Senate, Her Majesty, in the words of Hansard, was "pleased to deliver" the following speech:

> The first section of the Constitution of the Commonwealth of Australia provides that the legislative power of the Commonwealth shall be vested in 'a Federal Parliament, which shall consist of the Queen, a Senate and a House of Representatives'. It is therefore a joy for me, today, to address you not as a Queen from far away, but as your Queen and a part of your Parliament. In a real sense, you are here as my colleagues, friends and advisers.
>
> When I add to this consideration the fact that I am the first ruling Sovereign to visit Australia, it is clear that the events of today make a piece of history which fills me with deep pride and the most heartfelt pleasure, and which I am confident

> will serve to strengthen in your own hearts and minds a feeling of comradeship with the Crown and that sense of duty shared which we must all have as we confront our common tasks. [81]

Annabelle was unusually active as a contributor to debate in the Senate for the rest of the year. As a busy whip she mainly organised others to speak confining her own role to the occasional question on a matter of particular interest. In August she was given the honour usually reserved for newly-elected members of moving the motion that the Address-in-Reply to the Governor-General's Speech following the May election that year be agreed to.

In September, she rose to speak in the Budget debate. She built her speech around a theme of the 'people's budget' because of its strong focus on the welfare of the people of Australia. Before the end of the year she added her voice to the debate on the Aged Persons Homes Bill, congratulating her government for introducing the legislation and heartily agreeing with her Senate colleague Dorothy Tangney who had spoken before her:

> This is legislation of a kind for which I personally have longed for a considerable time. As my colleagues know, I have spoken on this subject on previous occasions. In my view, housing for aged people is one of the things that we require most.[82]

The following year Annabelle had to face re-election

for the first time since the 1951 double dissolution in which 10 Queensland Senators were elected. In 1955 her position was less assured because there were only the usual five Queensland Senators to be elected and she was still third below Cooper and O'Sullivan on the joint Coalition ticket. The Coalition had to achieve a large enough vote overall to ensure that she, and not the third ALP candidate, got the fifth Queensland Senate position. On the day, the Coalition's first preference vote was far ahead of that for Labor so Annabelle did not need the 16,886 first preference votes she attracted in her own right to be elected.

Changes to Senate voting introduced in 1948 had evolved into a new pattern. The former winner-takes-all with unbalanced outcomes such as an opposition with only three Senators as was the case from 1946 to 1949, and had been earlier in the 1930s, was replaced. Under the new system five Senators were elected from each State at an election for half the Senate. The first two on the Coalition and Labor ballot papers could be confident of election, leaving the fifth place to be fought over.

Women Senators often found themselves relegated to third on their own party ticket with a sometimes uncertain outcome. In 1955 Annabelle was safely elected because the Queensland vote to the Coalition was consistently and considerably higher than that for Labor.

Annabelle's next six-year term from 1956 to 1961

contained marked highs and lows with the most significant of the former coming when she was honoured in the Queen's Birthday Honours List of June 1957, ten years since she entered the Senate. Thereafter she was formally known as Dame Annabelle, Dame Commander of the Order of the British Empire, very appropriately for such a loyal daughter of the British-sphere. The congratulations which poured in are stored for posterity in bulging files in the Australian Archives.

Typical was the handwritten missive from one of her original Queensland Liberal Party supporters, Dr Winston Noble, soon to become a Queensland Government minister. "No one could have more fully deserved the honour bestowed on you. Personally, I would like to see it bestowed on you by the Queen in Person which would be a just reward for all you have done for the Nation," he wrote. Another from Senate colleague Nancy Buttfield may have caused the new Dame to raise an eyebrow, "We who work with you in the Senate know only too well what an arduous task you have and how exceptionally well you carry it out".[83]

In the second half of 1957 the Senate uncharacteristically became the focus of national attention. On this occasion the issue at stake was not a point of procedure or legal obscurity of little interest outside the Senate itself. It concerned one of the major points of contention and ideological difference between the two major political groupings. This was banking, including the future of the Commonwealth Bank.

Although the Australian Labor Party was fracturing ideologically over attitudes to Communism, banking was a different matter. Memories of Labor Government failure during the 1930s depression and efforts of the increasingly beatified Ben Chifley to place banking under government control were still burning strongly in the minds of Labor politicians, whether they were still in the official ALP or in one of its off-shoots which were yet to coalesce as the DLP – Democratic Labor Party.

Menzies biographer, Allan Martin, described how the banking issue came to a head:

> Always – once in power – relaxed on the banking issue Menzies ... was nevertheless constantly pressed by some of his backbenchers to carry 'reform' forward. Though masterful in his delaying tactics, he finally agreed to a series of conferences between the private banks, the Commonwealth Bank and the Treasury to explore the question, unresolved since 1949, of the relationship between the Commonwealth Bank, as a central bank, and the private banks ... The outcome of these talks, followed as they were by intensive Cabinet discussions, was a comprehensive package of 14 bills introduced into the (House of) Representatives by (Treasurer) Fadden, late in October.[84]

By mid-November the banking legislation and other bills were threatening to create a bottleneck in the Senate. Annabelle's Boswell at the *Courier-Mail* described the looming legislative logjam in his weekend "This Week in Canberra" column headed, "She Kept the Senate going with 41 Pins". He wrote:

> There were 41 pins in Senator Dame Annabelle Rankin's 'pin-up' board this week – more than ever before – and each one pinned up a Bill. This is the board which, as Senate Government Whip, she uses to keep track of the Senate's business. On Wednesday everything went wrong. Opposition Senators were adopting delaying tactics with long speeches in the Budget debate and Government Senators were threatening to retaliate with further delays.
>
> 'This is one of my worst days', declared Senator Rankin at 10 o'clock. 'I cannot see how we can get the new business in by half-past ten'. For 10.30pm is the Senate deadline for new business.
>
> But the auburn-haired Senator persevered, tactfully switched speakers, sweetly shunted Ministers and Senators into the chamber, rearranged business and had the right man up on the right Bill at 10.28pm.
>
> It was a very tired Senator who retired to her hotel bedroom at a few minutes before 1am – but that is just a day in the life of a Government Senate Whip.[85]

The Senate battle over the banking bills had been foreshadowed in the lower house. Allan Martin recorded, "Labor took the view that the legislation represented a 'sinister sellout' to private interests of the People's Bank, which had been neutralised during the Great Depression and restored in the great days of Chifley. So, on both sides, the past weighed heavily on the present".[86]

With the Bills through the House of Representatives, the Menzies Government had every prospect of similar success in the Senate because four Labor Senators including Senator Tangney were sick. Three of the sick Labor Senators were able to return to Canberra, however, and make their own way into the chamber to vote. A fourth, Senator Arnold, needed a wheelchair.

Summing up the unprecedented events in the Senate in his "This week in Canberra" column Elgin Reid wrote:

> The Senate this week was a battlefield. There was a war not only of votes but of nerves and feelings. Whether the responsibility of Senator Arnold's wheelchair presence in the House lay with the government or the opposition, a large number of Senators of both sides were very unhappy and uneasy...Senator Rankin, who had the unhappy responsibility of Government Whip, stuck it out like a soldier. But her feet betrayed her tenseness as, beneath her desk she shed one shoe, then the other, put them on, then off again, then on.[87]

The Menzies Government had miscalculated Labor's

determination to block the banking bills. The Senate Hansard for 27 November 1957 shows how in the procedural vote to bring on a division on the actual legislation – *Reserve Bank Bill 1957* and *Commonwealth Banks Bill 1957* – the voting was Ayes 28, Noes 27, so resolved in the affirmative.

But when the votes on the two Bills themselves were called, the ailing Senator Arnold was wheeled into the chamber. With his vote plus the three other sick Labor Senators and three anti-communist labour Senators, the vote was tied when the Senate divided: Ayes 28, Noes 28, Majority 0. In keeping with Senate rules, the question was resolved in the negative and the vote lost. The outcome was the same for the other twelve Banking Bills when they were considered later.[88] As Menzies' biographer noted:

> When the Bills reached the Senate, tradition briefly reasserted itself and the three anti-communist labour members voted with the Labor Party to reject them. Thus equally divided, the Senate in effect rejected the legislation, and it fell to the ground. The same thing happened when the bills were brought up again in the first half of 1958. Menzies might then have requested a double dissolution. But he chose not to, contenting himself with the observation that 'the Australian electors will have a golden opportunity when next they vote to cast a Senate vote which will prevent the views of the lower house from being frustrated.[89]

The next golden opportunity was towards the end of 1958, when a clear majority of Australian electors cast their votes for the Coalition, increasing the Menzies Government's number of seats in the lower house and returning a government majority in the Senate. Annabelle did not have to face the voters but there were expectations that she would get a ministry in the post-election reshuffle.

After earlier elections her name had occasionally cropped up in the Queensland press as a ministerial possibility. This time her appointment appeared to be a probability particularly as a fellow Queensland Senator was vacating his ministerial position. Menzies, however, chose Victorian Senator John Gorton instead. Gorton's biographer wrote:

> If, as expected, Senator Neil O'Sullivan was either dropped or retired, his most likely replacement from the Senate was thought to be Annabelle Rankin (Qld), the government whip, who had first entered the Senate in 1946. Other names cropped up as the date for a ministerial announcement grew closer, but Gorton's name was not among them. When Menzies announced on 8 December that he would be Minister for the Navy, replacing Senator O'Sullivan, the press treated the appointment as 'the big surprise'. Rankin, 'the popular tip', had missed out.[90]

Luck was not running her way. Towards the end of 1959 she contracted the painful nerve condition, shingles. Her illness was so severe she was in hospital for several weeks and temporarily lost vision in one eye.

In 1961 Annabelle's six-year term was up and she faced re-election. Although Senator O'Sullivan's resignation from the ministry did not lead to her becoming a minister, it did result in her being placed second on the joint Country-Liberal Party ballot paper in Queensland. She was not personally affected by the big swing against the Coalition which nearly unseated the Menzies Government in the election that year. Eight of her Queensland colleagues in the House of Representatives lost their seats, but not including her Brisbane friend Jim Killen whose close victory in the electorate of Moreton famously provided the Menzies Government with its one seat majority.

When the new Senators from the 1961 election took their places in July of the following year, the Menzies Government's majority was a slim two, giving Annabelle little respite in her ongoing role as Government Whip. She rarely spoke in the Senate at this time but her contribution to the Budget debate in May 1963 shows that her electorate work was undiminished as was her direct interest in a wide range of family, health, and welfare issues.

Annabelle always kept a close watch on the small appropriation of only a few thousand dollars in the Commonwealth Budget for the emergency housekeeper service. The funding had remained static for many years and she thought it was due for an increase. Speaking in the Budget debate, she said, "Today, we see, over and over again, the problem of a family from which the mother is taken to hospital for treatment; it is a great problem".[91]

Her next topic was the need for more help for civilian widows which was also a preoccupation of Senator Ivy Wedgewood who was in the chamber interjecting her support. Annabelle recommended a new allowance:

> Year after year, she (the civilian widow) faces great hardship and very great problems. I should like the government to give further consideration to this problem. I suggest that, if it is possible, the civilian widow be assisted by a domestic allowance which could be varied according to the number of children.[92]

Changing tack Annabelle turned to "another subject which is very near to my heart...I almost mention the word with bated breath, because I think honourable Senators know what it will be."

"Geriatrics", interjected Senator Tangney from the other side of the chamber.

"Correct", responded Annabelle going on to commend the current Minister for Repatriation who had recently opened the geriatric wing for ex-servicemen in a Brisbane hospital for which she had long been campaigning. She then moved on to rehabilitation of disabled children calling for a dedicated centre in Townsville so those afflicted would not need to travel the considerable distance to Brisbane for treatment.[93]

Later in 1963 Prime Minister Menzies took advantage of internal divisions in the Labor Party to hold a House of Representatives only election in November, a year earlier than it was due. The gamble paid off with a handsome 22 seat majority in the lower house including the return of three of the eight seats lost in Queensland. Menzies' biographer explained:

> Liberal domestic policy at the end of the 1963 election had been in part consciously shaped to meet the needs of younger married couples, with the promise of a housing subsidy scheme for persons up to the age of 35, as well as the educational improvements entailed in the extension of Commonwealth aid to all schools.[94]

The wheel had turned. Demographic trends dictated that young people were the group the Liberal Party needed to attract, replacing women who had been an earlier target of attention. Part of the new look government following the 1963 election was a dedicated housing ministry, one of three new portfolios and seven ministerial changes, including five new ministers under 50 years of age. Annabelle, now in her mid-50s, was not among them.

Minister for Housing

Annabelle achieved her ambition to enter the Ministry in 1966. Her pride on her swearing in as Minister for Housing in new Prime Minister Harold Holt's first ministry at Government House on Australia Day, 26 January 1966 is recorded in her biography:

> I was so delighted that it was Australia Day, that my Prime Minister, Harold Holt, was an Australian and that Lord Casey, Governor-General, was an Australian; and as I look back, that my other colleague for the swearing in, Malcolm Fraser, was to become Prime Minister of Australia. This was a truly historic occasion. Such occasions one never forgets. Of course, it was quite nerve-wracking. I remember being very nervous about it and then after it was all over wondering why I had worried.[95]

Former Prime Minister Robert Menzies had retired at the start of 1966. New Prime Minister Harold Holt maintained the ministerial team he had inherited with only two additions, one of whom was Annabelle, in his first ministry.

The positive domestic achievements Holt is best remembered for are supporting and expanding the 1967 Aboriginal referendum and, in relation to immigration, working towards ending the White Australia. Holt also struck two blows for women. As well as appointing Annabelle as the first woman with ministerial responsibility for administering a government department, he introduced legislation to remove the ban on married women holding permanent positions in the Commonwealth Public Service which had been recommended by the 1959 Boyer *Committee of Inquiry into Public Service Recruitment.*

Once the celebrations and ceremonials were over Annabelle had little over a month until Parliament resumed and she was to move from the seat in the second row she had occupied as Whip for 15 years to take her place as the first woman on a Senate front bench.

She had taken a close interest in housing since her first election campaign and regularly participated in debate on housing and related topics. This was fortuitous because she had to introduce and hopefully successfully carry through the Senate two important pieces of housing legislation as soon as Parliament resumed. Housing may have been a junior portfolio, but it was a nationally significant marker of economic activity. Any housing shortage or fall off in home construction activity quickly became a major issue and this was one of the challenges facing the first Holt government, as Holt biographer Tom Frame observed:

> There was evidence of a slight increase in unemployment, real wages were declining, housing approvals were down and the growth in gross domestic product was minimal. Sections

of the media noted that that Australia's 'stop-go' economy had 'come to a Holt.'[96]

Menzies had recognised the economic and political importance of housing following the 1963 election by establishing a stand-alone Department of Housing. As Minister he appointed the competent but uncharismatic Leslie Bury, a returning Minister who had been demoted to the backbench after he criticised his own government's approach to Britain's entry into the European Economic Community. The task of establishing the department's administration was given to respected Treasury official, James F. Nimmo.

A business newsletter profile on Annabelle after a year as Minister reported, "Mr Nimmo's health was endangered in the early hectic days of the formation and planning of the Department of Housing. He worked exceedingly hard with few resources, but is now better equipped, for the process of building his team is now well under way." Of the Minister, the author wrote, "…with the initial work done she has handled her job solidly and has probably made many friends for herself and for the Holt Government by introducing to the Department a measure of discretion which did not exist in Mr Bury's time. Dame Annabelle has been openly sympathetic in the exercise of this discretionary power".[97]

That Annabelle would exercise her ministerial discretion fulsomely and sympathetically would have been no surprise to anyone who had listened to her many speeches in the Senate advocating on behalf of those less fortunate. She also brought to her role the energy and empathy which had made her so popular as speaker and guest of honour at events throughout Queensland.

Well in advance of the election due towards the end of 1966 a prominent photograph of her with her distinctive hairstyle featuring a white quiff was adorning booklets promoting the Home Savings Grant Scheme with "A message to the young people in Australia":

> This pamphlet is designed to help you take advantage of the Commonwealth Government's offer of a Home Savings Grant of up to $500 when you come to buy or build the first home you own after you marry.
>
> The Grant is a tax-free gift to young married people who have saved for their home in the manner required under the Scheme and have met the other requirements explained in the pamphlet.
>
> There is a message for all young people in this pamphlet – whether you are a young husband or wife, a young widow or widower, a young unmarried person or even a boy or girl still at school.[98]

The Home Savings Grant Scheme was not the most important program the housing department administered but it had a high profile and was popular with Liberal backbenchers. Don Cameron who became the Liberal Member for the Brisbane electorate of Griffith at the 1966 election used to monitor the Brisbane newspapers for wedding announcements so he could send the happy couple his congratulations together with a copy of Annabelle's home savings grant pamphlet.[99]

As soon as parliamentary sittings began for the year in March, Annabelle's priorities were the *Loans (Housing) Bill* to approve the injection of a much needed $15 million to the States to boost housing activity and the *Housing Agreements Bill* to enable a further five-year extension of the *Commonwealth-State Housing Agreement*. The agreement was the principal legal avenue for the Commonwealth to make funds available to the States for the construction of public housing and lending of funds for home purchase.

In her first session as Minister from March to May, Annabelle also had to introduce an additional five pieces of legislation for other ministers whom she represented in the Senate. They were *Aliens, Migration and Nationality and Citizenship bills* for the Minister for Immigration and the *Quarantine and Therapeutic Goods Bills* for the Minister for Health.

In her own portfolio the sharp point of political contention was government funding for private home ownership. The original housing agreement introduced by the Chifley Government was for rental dwellings only. The agreements from 1956 to 1973 when a

Coalition Government was in power were aimed at encouraging home ownership by providing low interest loans to home builders and the sale of houses on highly concessional terms while still funding public housing and accommodation for newly arrived migrants.

Home ownership was a cornerstone of the Menzies Liberal philosophy in both actual and philosophical terms. Owning your own home embodied individual choice and free enterprise as well as a reward for effort, thrift and persistence.

Labor vehemently opposed the Coalition's approach to housing. For the old trade unionists still present in Labor's Senate ranks the focus on home ownership was a prime example of the evils of capitalism over socialism. There was an underlying belief that any profit from the sale of land should be returned to the community, not benefit individuals. In addition, the Coalition's housing policy and programs of home ownership and working in co-operation with the states were a negation of the Chifley government's national approach focussing totally on publicly-owned housing. An element of Labor still subscribed to the former Labor Minister John Dedman's observation in relation to the first *Commonwealth State Housing Agreement*, "The Commonwealth Government ... is not concerned with making the workers into little capitalists".[100]

For Annabelle the political and ideological divisions

on housing meant that Labor contested every housing measure that came before parliament, often moving substantial amendments which involved long hours of debate and contested votes in the chamber.

Her tenure as Minister for Housing began nevertheless on a positive and supportive note. The first words she uttered were in answer to a question from fellow Liberal Senator Dame Ivy Wedgewood on the Home Savings Grant Scheme which was a signature Liberal Party program. Then in the course of debate on the first legislation she introduced, her ministerial advent was warmly welcomed by the more recently arrived woman Liberal Senator from Victoria Marie Breen. Speaking in support of the *Loan (Housing Bill)*, Senator Breen said she did so with pleasure as it was the first Bill presented by Annabelle:

> Dame Annabelle's appointment to this portfolio was greeted throughout Australia with very great pleasure indeed and, may I say, more particularly by the women with whom she worked in her own state of Queensland and all the associated women's organisations in other states, members of which have followed her splendid career throughout the years.[101]

The Australian Labor Party Opposition, did not greet the Bill with any pleasure at all. Labor moved an amendment to establish a Senate Select Committee to investigate all aspects of the Bill because "the existing Housing

Agreement has not fully met the housing requirements of the Australian people".[102] The proposed committee was also to investigate rental rebates, slum clearance, housing for pensioners, land development and town planning.

Labor speakers stressed they were not opposed to the extra funds for the States but did use their amendment as a way of pointing out that failure to meet housing needs was an indictment on the government with adverse effects on the whole economy. The Democratic Labor Party's two Senators did not support the amendment because the $15 million would be a shot in the arm for an industry which had been under a cloud and the Bill was approved by the Senate with a comfortable majority of five. Labor mounted a more serious attack on the *Housing Agreement Bill* which was to extend the Commonwealth State Housing Agreement for a further five years. The main Labor speaker was the Leader of the Opposition, Senator Nick McKenna, who had been a Chifley minister, and was a formidable debater.

The Labor amendments went to the heart of the fundamental disagreement over housing policy as well as reprising the previous advocacy for slum clearance, land development and town planning. The first and most important amendment proposed increasing the annual payment to the states by "amounts equal to those allocated in the current financial year to building societies".[103] As payments to building societies were the principal avenue for providing funding for home ownership Labor was attempting to restore to public housing the level of funding which had applied when it was previously in government. Although this legislation related to the highest level of policy and finance for housing, Annabelle ensured that her longstanding concern for appropriate housing for the aged at reasonable rental was not forgotten. As she told the Senate, "We are not ignorant of the fact that some of our elderly citizens are suffering hardships because they are living under wretched conditions. These things concern each and every one of us".[104]

The House of Representatives election in November 1966 was a triumph for the Coalition, but 1967 was a better year for Annabelle than for the Holt Government. The 1966 election left the Holt Government with the largest majority ever recorded in the House of Representatives at that time. Early the following year however Gough Whitlam became Leader of the Opposition and a series of electoral, political and parliamentary reverses damaged the Holt Government's standing. Two by-elections were lost and the vote for the Coalition at the half Senate election towards the end of the year was seven per cent below that in the lower house poll the previous year.

There were also two damaging military scandals. A second royal commission into the sinking of HMAS Voyager[105] was followed by the mishandling of questions about use of the RAAF VIP squadron. Discord was apparent in ministerial ranks with antagonism between Country

Party leader Jack McEwen and Treasurer William McMahon. The Holt Government was also vulnerable in the Senate with the ALP and DLP combining repeatedly to reject rises in postal charges.

While Annabelle had a good year behind the scenes, on the floor of the Senate she was back in the trenches. The Opposition attacked changes to the *Aged Persons Homes Bill 1967* to widen the eligibility criteria to allow local governing bodies to receive and disburse funds for aged housing which had been promised in Harold Holt's 1966 election policy speech. The ALP moved an amendment to further widen eligibility to trade unions and with DLP support the amendment was carried with a slim majority of two. With its popularity faltering and a half-Senate election due, the Government had no intention of giving way on this issue despite DLP support.

The House of Representatives rejected the amendment and sent the legislation back to the Senate in its original form in the second half of the year. After many speeches in which the most repeated phrase was "storm in a teacup", the original version was passed on the voices without a vote but only after Annabelle had provided assurance that if a trade union applied to be an aged persons home provider it would be eligible under the Act or could become eligible by setting up an appropriate trust.[106]

Some years later Annabelle recalled how she used to break such deadlocks by,"...talking to my friend Condon

Byrne and other members of the DLP and they came and we worked on that oh for hours into the night, into the early morning, and we found a place where we could find a point of agreement, and they were happy and I was happy and we got the Bill through."[107]

Annabelle had good reason for satisfaction away from the public gaze. She was enjoying the confidence of the Prime Minister, her leader. In August, Holt asked her to be one of his representatives on the Federal Campaign Committee for the upcoming half Senate election and in October she submitted at the Prime Minister's request a Cabinet submission to address the housing problems of the most needy in the community. Headed "Personal", Annabelle sent the following hand-written letter:

> My dear PM
>
> I have done my homework as requested by you, on my ideas for housing the needy. Also as requested officers of my department consulted officers of the Treasury and Social Services in the preparation of this submission. Enclosed is a copy of the submission which has been sent to the Cabinet Office for distribution.
>
> Kind personal regards
>
> Annabelle J. Rankin[108]

Housing, particularly for the aged, had been a preoccupation of Annabelle's throughout her political career. As she subsequently told an interviewer, "The housing of the aged had always been a particular worry of mine because I felt that people spent so much money on very poor accommodation and had so little left from their pension to meet the other needs".[109] This view was informed by expeditions Annabelle had undertaken herself on foot and wearing dark glasses to deprived housing areas in Sydney, together with her first-hand knowledge of conditions in Queensland.[110]

The submission she lodged in the prescribed manner with the word "Confidential" at the top and bottom of every page was not formally expressed in customary bureaucratic language. Even the title – *Housing Assistance to the Really Needy* – reflected Annabelle's own style. As Annabelle stated in the opening paragraph of her submission:

> Although we have done a great deal in recent years to improve the housing and living conditions of pensioners, I sense a feeling in the community that the Government should be showing more interest in the condition of the relatively few who are still living in miserable circumstances, and that we should do something special and additional in the housing field to improve their lot.[111]

According to the departments of Housing and Social Services those most in need were among the aged and invalid pensioners, widows and deserted wives with dependent children and large low-income families.

"Our broad programmes for social welfare provide for the minimum reasonable needs of the many, but not for the minimum reasonable needs of everyone. It is the few whose reasonable minimum needs are not being met and who are not adequately housed that are the cause for concern," her submission said.[112]

All other housing efforts of the Commonwealth and the States were not reducing the waiting lists for aged persons' units. The waiting period for single person units was five years in New South Wales, four years in Victoria and seven years in South Australia. Obviously, there was a substantial shortage of single person units.

Annabelle began her concluding paragraph by stating she felt strongly that, "the provision of some special assistance in raising the standard of living of the most miserably housed aged persons, and widows and deserted wives with dependent children is action that should be taken". The first and most important recommendation of Annabelle's housing submission called for Cabinet to approve, "that we offer the States advances of at least $5 million per annum for the next five years for the construction of self-contained units suitable for those elderly citizens capable of looking after themselves and most in need of reasonable minimum accommodation at a modest rental".[113]

The last weeks of 1967 were busy but rewarding for Annabelle. She finalised her *Housing Assistance to the Really*

Needy Cabinet submission and negotiated the successful passage of the *Aged Persons Homes Bill* through the Senate, without specific mention of trade unions, before the end of October.

The half-Senate election was held on 25 November 1967 and Annabelle was accorded the honour of first place on the combined Liberal-Country Party Senate voting ballot paper in Queensland. While she was assured of re-election the poll was disappointing for the Holt Government. Queensland Senate voting showed how far support for the Coalition federally had slipped since the 1950s when the Liberal-Country parties were assured of three Senate seats. The vote for the ALP in 1967 was well ahead of that for the Coalition parties despite the DLP recording around a tenth of the first preference votes and winning the fifth Senate seat.

Annabelle's star was in the ascendancy. She was re-appointed to the ministry after the Senate election and in her home state she had been placed above the Country Party on the Senate ballot paper, a rare occurrence. She had been a successful minister who had the confidence of her Prime Minister and she could look forward to having her own proposal considered by Cabinet in the new year

The hand-written letter accompanying her housing submission that Annabelle sent to Harold Holt was dated 17 October 1967. Two months later to the day – 17 December 1967 – Harold Holt was dead, drowned off

Portsea in Victoria. Annabelle learnt of the tragedy in the midst of hosting a Christmas party for her staff.

John Gorton became leader of the Liberal Party and Prime Minister in January the following year. Not surprisingly Annabelle retained her ministry under Gorton. She had worked with him in the Senate, and he enjoyed her respect for his war service, especially as he had been shot down and wounded as a pilot. Her oral history in the National Library records her saying, "I had great admiration for John Gorton, and great admiration for the way he cared for people".[114]

In the early part of the year she went to Mauritius, leading the official Australian group to the former British colony's celebration of independence. She was the only woman to be representing her country as head of a delegation.

Later that year she became one of three joint "fathers" of the Senate along with two others elected in 1946. This came about when the previous longest serving Senator Dorothy Tangney had to leave not by choice but because she had lost her party's support. Annabelle was sorry to see her go. In her valedictory speech on 13 June Annabelle revealed why she had reached out across the aisle to Tangney in her maiden speech twenty-one years earlier:

> I remember the first thing Dorothy ever said to me. It was in the Parliamentary Library. She came up to me and said, 'I am Dorothy Tangney. Can I do anything to help you?' ... I think that she may have

forgotten it, but I have not.¹¹⁵

Before the end of the parliamentary year Annabelle introduced a *War Service Homes Bill* to increase the maximum loan former service people could borrow to $8,000 from the $7,000 it had been since 1962. She also introduced the annual *Loan (Housing) Bill* which increased the amount being advanced to the states for housing purposes by 2.5 per cent to $126 million. With building construction rates continuing to rise and the rate of home ownership now above 70 per cent of householders, the Opposition raised no objections.

Meanwhile what had happened to Annabelle's Cabinet submission on housing assistance to the really needy? As she recalled in her biography:

> I put a scheme to Cabinet which, because of other needs of the day, was rejected. Although disappointed, because of my loyalty to my leader, and I believed that Cabinet had good advice, I accepted the decision, but was determined that I would come back again with my submission. This I did and although I had several knock-backs I finally received the full support of Cabinet and money was provided for housing for single aged people.¹¹⁶

Annabelle's success was announced officially in the Treasurer's Budget Speech in August 1969:

> We recognise that the housing of some single age and service pensioners with little or no means

> apart from their pension is below acceptable standards and the rentals they are required to pay are excessive. The States are already providing self-contained dwelling units including units for single age pensioners at reasonable rentals. We believe that more should be done and therefore propose to offer to the States non-repayable grants of $25 million over five years, beginning this year, so that building of this type of dwelling can be expedited.[117]

Annabelle had displayed considerable determination and political acumen in repeatedly pressing for her submission for housing assistance to the really needy to be considered and reconsidered. A year after she had successfully had her proposal agreed in the 1969 Budget she was able to give the Senate an update and, thanks to an interjecting Labor Senator, she was able to proudly provide more details than she had originally intended:

> **Senator Dame Annabelle Rankin** – In September last year we authorised a grant of $25 million to be paid over five years to the States for dwellings for single aged pensioners. It is estimated that in 1970-71, $5.7 million of that sum will be paid to the States for the erection of such dwellings. The housing needs of many single aged pensioners are indeed urgent and I exhort the States to proceed with the construction of more dwellings for these pensioners as rapidly as possible.
>
> **Senator Hendrickson** – Where have you started them?

Senator Dame Annabelle Rankin – They have been started in NSW, Victoria, South Australia, Western Australia and Tasmania.

Senator Hendrickson – What part of Victoria?

Senator Dame Annabelle Rankin – I can give the honourable Senator a list.

Senator Hendrickson – They are for pensioners?

Senator Dame Annabelle Rankin – They are for eligible single age pensioners...

Senator Hendrickson – At what rental?

Senator Dame Annabelle Rankin – From memory the rentals vary from $2 to $3.20. That is in my notes but I should like to check it.

Senator Hendrickson – I should like the information.

Senator Dame Annabelle Rankin – I would be very glad to give it to you. I was pleased to have the opportunity to open in Hobart the first units that were made available. All the States have accepted gladly this assistance because they recognise the very great need that exists for single pensioner dwellings. The States either have commenced construction of the dwellings, have already built them or have told us of their plans and are awaiting approval for commencement during this financial year.[118]

Shortly thereafter she travelled to all the State capitals unveiling foundation stones commemorating the opening of the first single pensioner dwellings in each location.

Now, after a quarter of a century in the Senate and five as Minister for Housing, it was time for Annabelle to look to the future. Sometime earlier William McMahon, who became Foreign Minister in November 1969, offered her a diplomatic post but she asked for the appointment to be deferred because of her outstanding commitments including single aged pensioner housing. Developing political events intervened making Annabelle's transition from political to diplomatic life less smooth than originally planned.

Annabelle was one of a select band of his colleagues who had a good word to say about McMahon. She had encountered him early in his ministerial career when he was Minister for Social Services in the 1950s and found him sympathetic towards the plight of handicapped children, an attitude guaranteed to impress Annabelle.

The growing antagonism between Gorton and McMahon placed her in a difficult position. Like many of her Queensland Liberal colleagues, particularly Jim Killen, she was a loyal supporter of Gorton. There was however a powerful faction in the Queensland Liberal Party organisational wing strongly supporting McMahon, including by pressuring parliamentarians to vote for him in party ballots. McMahon together with another minister had unsuccessfully challenged Gorton's leadership shortly after the 1969 election.

Neither Holt nor Gorton was able to provide the stable

leadership or stamp their authority over their Liberal colleagues as Menzies had done. Gorton had defeated one challenge to his leadership, but it was far from clear if he would still be leading the government which faced an increasingly confident Labor Party under Whitlam at the next election due in 1972. Was Annabelle willing to face the prospect of going into opposition again?

A diplomat and final years

William McMahon took over from Gorton in March 1971. As his biographer Patrick Mullins recorded:

> On 21 March, McMahon took the list of his ministry to Government House for Hasluck's approval. There were predictable names on the list ... There were also notable absences: Malcolm Fraser had been left on the backbench, and Senator Annabelle Rankin, who had burst into tears when told she was out, had a diplomatic posting to New Zealand as consolation.[119]

Annabelle had been travelling around Australia promoting her housing for aged singles program, when the simmering Liberal Party leadership tensions boiled over, leading to the demise of Gorton. Annabelle's future had not been decided before then and she was still Minister for Housing until 22 March when all the other numerous changes to the ministry were announced. She wrote to the Governor-General to resign as a Senator for

Queensland two days later on 24 May.[120]

The eleven days between McMahon's accession to the leadership and announcing his new team were full of tension and uncertainty for all concerned, particularly Annabelle. Another Queenslander who had supported Gorton was Jim Killen who was despatched to the backbench, learning of his fate on 18 March. Annabelle never divulged exactly when she learnt she was going to New Zealand except to tell her last interviewer that she was "thrilled" when she heard the news.[121]

On the basis of previous evidence, it is highly likely Annabelle did shed tears on learning of her future but they were more likely to have been tears of relief than of anger or disappointment. To her, New Zealand was not a consolation prize, it was the first prize. Second prize would have been to continue on as a minister with little opportunity for new policy initiatives and third prize, a humiliating return to the backbench. Her previously observed tearful episodes also occurred after periods of frustration and anxiety but in front of sympathetic audiences, Enid Lyons and Hubert Opperman. Whoever revealed her March 1971 tears wanted to hurt, not heal.

Annabelle had already left the Senate when the traditional valedictory speeches were made at the end of the session. Some of the most laudatory tributes to Annabelle came from the other sides of politics. Opposition Leader Senator Lionel Murphy highlighted the longevity of her service to the Senate, noting that she held the distinction of being the last member of the government who had also been in opposition. Her fellow Queenslander the DLP Senator Byrne revealed one of the secrets of her success as government Whip whereby she, "always provided midnight suppers for honourable Senators whose tempers were frayed and were brought to any discharge of their duties only by the solicitude she always showed in the discharge of her duties". Byrne added that in her time as a Senator Annabelle had witnessed the Senate develop from a, "rubber stamp into a viable and purposeful forum for the States and the Commonwealth".[122]

A month later on 6 June Annabelle flew to the New Zealand capital, Wellington. Waiting for her was the Deputy High Commissioner, John Melhuish, who shared his frank recollection with the ABC:

> I can remember quite clearly waiting at the Wellington airport to welcome Dame Annabelle Rankin. I had lots of misgivings at the time. She was the first woman to be appointed as a High Commissioner and I wondered just how well a woman would do the job. I also wondered whether she would be tired or worn out as a result of her long parliamentary career. Well, the airport was awful that night. It was late and it was cold and it was wet but she bounced off the plane full of zest and had a tonic effect on all of us.[123]

There were other unstated elements at play on both sides

of that first meeting. Professional foreign affairs officials do not like political appointments. Former politicians filling top diplomatic posts undermines their career prospects and as in any closed group there is antipathy to outsiders. As Annabelle conceded later, she felt "very lonely" on the way to New Zealand. For the previous twenty years she had the comforting knowledge that wherever her travels took her she would return to her sister and her mother in their Brisbane River-side house in Toowong. In Canberra she had a supportive ministerial staff including a private secretary, now known as chief of staff, and a press secretary occupying her familiar M51 offices off Kings Hall with a view into the Senate courtyard.[124]

Annabelle appears to have overcome the reservations of the public servants staffing the High Commission with her usual blend of hard work and charm. She also totally redecorated the High Commission's premises which improved their working conditions. For his part Melhuish and his wife did more than the official duties required in helping Annabelle adjust to her new role. Whatever residual loneliness she felt on arrival was dispelled by the consideration of her diplomatic staff and the volume of work.

On the political front there were changes of government on both sides of the Tasman. Britain's entry to the European Union in 1972 had a bigger impact on New

Zealand than Australia. New Zealand sent two of its navy ships to protest against French nuclear testing on Moruroa Atoll in the Pacific and the Commonwealth Games were held in Christchurch in 1974.

In her term of more than three years, she had two Australian prime ministers and four New Zealanders including incoming NZ Labor PM Norman Kirk who died in office while she was there. Events on the water and on ships consistently featured on her schedules. Despite fears of sea sickness she boarded HMAS Sydney which was transporting Australian soldiers to training in New Zealand, inspected two visiting Australian National Line ships, sailed from Wellington to Auckland on HMAS Stalwart, started a Trans-Tasman yacht race and dined with the Queen on the royal yacht *HMS Britannia* when it was in New Zealand waters for the Christchurch Commonwealth Games.

After she returned to Australia at the conclusion of her extended term as High Commissioner to New Zealand in September 1974, Annabelle set about restoring order to her personal life and ensuring her legacy. Preparation had already been made for where she would live. She and her sister Jean, similarly unmarried, had bought adjoining house blocks at Deception Bay at the seaside north of Brisbane. Jean had already built her home and Annabelle needed to sell her Brisbane house as well as building her own new home next to her sister. Their mother – Annabelle senior - lived to be 99 and her two daughters cared for her until she died in 1978.

Annabelle had gone straight from being Minister for Housing to New Zealand and her personal and official papers needed attention. The Commonwealth Archives approached her about depositing her records but that was going to take time as her carefully collected and curated files and books of personal papers, photographs and newspaper clippings were voluminous. Her collection consists of more than 800 items. Non-officially plans were afoot for a biography, an ABC documentary tribute and, later, a National Library oral history.

The National Archives of Australia file on the deposit of her papers is substantial. Much of the correspondence consists of trivial administrative detail but on one point in particular Rankin was adamant. She was insistent that a copy of the ABC documentary appropriately entitled simply "Annabelle" and broadcast in May 1977 be incorporated in her collection. By viewing the video or reading the transcript it is clear why she wanted the 42-minute ABC program to be part of her legacy and to set the record straight on a number of issues.

Her retirement was an active one. Annabelle reconnected with the Girl Guides, the organisation to which she felt the greatest connection. She was invited to be the first woman on the Board of Governors for the Utah Development Corporation's charitable trust, another reminder of her formative years in Queensland. The US company operated five large coal mines in Queensland. She was also much in demand as a speaker, particularly by the Liberal Party.

After nearly three decades of public life Annabelle was candid in her ABC interview about what she did not miss in retirement, telling the interviewer, "I enjoy my house, I enjoy all the things that go with it. I enjoy getting into the car and driving somewhere and thinking 'Well I haven't got to be there at such and such a time'".[125]

In 1984 the new Federal electorate of Rankin in Queensland was named in her honour. She died two years later on 30 August 1986 shortly after her 78th birthday. She was accorded a State Funeral which was held at the Brisbane Anglican Cathedral.

Marking her death in the House of Representatives, the then Prime Minister Bob Hawke spoke of her record of considerable community service before she entered parliament and of the paramountcy she continued to give these concerns during her 25 years of parliamentary service. Echoing the title of her biography, *A Woman of Distinction*, the Prime Minister said:

> Dame Annabelle was a long-standing and respected member of the Senate and served her country and her party with distinction.[126]

Then Opposition Leader John Howard summed up her ground breaking "firsts" and pioneering involvement as a woman in Australian politics, concluding:

> By any measure and by whatever criterion of political belief or commitment, (hers) was a remarkable achievement ... Dame Annabelle's record is an impressive one for any Australian.[127]

Note on sources

Without this brief explanation readers would be puzzled about one of the main sources of information for this work particularly the non-standard references. The source material is a 42-minute ABC television documentary entitled "Annabelle" which was broadcast on 5 May 1977.

The documentary is crucial to this work because Annabelle Rankin herself and the other interviewees were more informative for this program than elsewhere. Dame Enid Lyons reveals previous untold personal details about Annabelle. Sir Charles Wanstall while still Chief Justice of Queensland identifies himself as the mystery 'party executive member' who convinced her to seek pre-selection and Charles Porter is remarkably frank about his party's state of preparation for the 1946 election campaign.

In the case of Annabelle herself, the interview for the documentary was recorded barely two years after she retired from public life. Her memory and her recollection are sharper than in subsequent interviews and oral histories.

The manner in which the ABC provided the documentary to National Archives and its subsequent cataloguing are problematic. The documentary is spread over two different series, the video in one and a transcript in another. This dual listing would not be a problem, but the video has been miscatalogued under "Children's Art" and the transcript has two sets of pagination, one at the top and the other at the bottom of each page.

As is recorded in "Dame Annabelle Rankin - Personal Archives", this came about because Annabelle specifically requested that the documentary be included in her papers and there is a paper trail of correspondence with archives central office repeatedly chasing up its Queensland office and the ABC in Brisbane to fulfill Annabelle's request.

To avoid confusion for readers and researchers I have departed from the usual practice of providing page numbers with the references to the ABC program. I have instead identified the interviewee. This should suffice because the transcript provided by the ABC is a broadcast version all in capitals with the speakers' name on the left hand side of the page (video) with what is being said (audio) on the right hand side.

National Archives of Australia has been approached about the cataloguing error and the ABC about providing NAA with permission to allow better access to this important historical document.

My thanks are due to Kate Armstrong of the Museum of Australian Democracy (Old Parliament House) for taking me to Annabelle's office and providing me with a copy of the photo of the Senate chamber when the Queen was there is 1954, and to Australian War Memorial military heraldry expert Shane Casey who identified Annabelle's service and civilian medals.

Former Queensland Liberal Members of the House of Representatives John Hodges and Don Cameron were generous with their memories. The Rankin family were John Hodges' constituents when they lived at Deception Bay and he was Member for Petrie. Don Cameron remembered how valuable the *Home Saving Grant Scheme* administered by Annabelle was to an MHR in a marginal electorate.

Endnotes

1. See Anne Henderson, *Margaret Guilfoyle*, Connor Court Publishing, Redland Bay, 2021
2. See Sean Jacobs, *Neville Bonner*, Connor Court Publishing, Redland Bay, 2021
3. Kathy Martin Sullivan MP, *Women in Parliament – Yes! But What's It Really Like?*, Papers on Parliament No. 22, February 1994, pp. 2-3.2021
4. Author, telephone conversation with owners, August 2022.
5. Frasercoast.qld.gov.au/local-heritage-register, August 2022.
6. Ibid.
7. Raymond L. Whitmore, 'Rankin, Colin Dunlop Wilson (1869–1940)', *Australian Dictionary of Biography*, National Centre of Biography, Australian National University, https://adb.anu.edu.au/biography/rankin-colin-dunlop-wilson-8155/text14251, published first in hardcopy 1988.
8. National Archives Australia (NAA), Personal Archives- Dame Annabelle Rankin CP137, A3437, A1986/477,11482079, Transcript of ABC Documentary "Annabelle" broadcast 5 May 1977 (see Note on Sources).
9. Waveney Browne, *A Woman of Distinction*, Boolarong Publications, Brisbane, 1981, pp. 12-14.
10. Sylvia Marchant, *Rankin, Dame Annabelle*, The Biographical Dictionary of the Senate, Vol 3, 1962-83, UNSW Press, Sydney, 2010, pp. 275-79.
11. Browne, *A Woman of Distinction*, p. 19.
12. Rupert Goodman, *Queensland Nurses Boer War to Vietnam*, Boolarong Publications, Brisbane, 1985, p. 186.
13. NAA, ABC, op.cit. – Charles Wanstall.
14. Queensland People's Party, (QPP), Newsletter, 1946; NAA, Dame Annabel Rankin, Scrapbook 1946, M2110,3, 1336246.
15. NAA, ABC, op.cit. – Enid Lyons.
16. Author telephone conversation with Robert Howse, son of John Howse, Member for Calare, June 2022.
17. NAA, ABC, op.cit. – Annabelle Rankin.
18. Ibid.
19. *Brisbane Telegraph*, 1946, NAA, Dame Annabel Rankin, Scrapbook 1946, M2110,3,1336246.

20. Annabelle Rankin, Oral History Interview, conducted by Pat Shaw, 1983-84, National Library of Australia (NLA).
21. NAA, ABC, op.cit. – Charles Porter.
22. QPP Newsletter, 1946.
23. "Miss Rankin Won Hearts of Audience", *Maryborough Chronicle*, 25 July 1946.
24. NAA, ABC, op.cit. – Charles Porter.
25. "Marriage Can Wait, Says 'Our Annabelle'", *Courier-Mail*, 28 August 1946.
26. NAA, ABC, op.cit. – Annabelle Rankin.
27. *Courier-Mail*, 'Marriage Can Wait", 28 August 1946.
28. *The Argus*, Melbourne, 24 August 1946.
29. NAA, ABC, op.cit. – James Killen.
30. "QPP Political Tea Party: Miss Rankin Welcomed", *The Daily Mercury*, Mackay, 29 August 1946.
31. NAA, Dame Annabelle Rankin-Political Speech, circa 1946. M1569,37,1336236.
32. Ibid.
33. Ibid.
34. Ibid.
35. *The Daily Telegraph*, Sydney, 20 August 1947.
36. *The Bulletin*, Sydney, 27 August 1947. The poet signed himself/herself as 'T the R'
37. NAA, Dame Annabelle Rankin-folder of newspaper clippings, 1947, M2110, 6, 1336247.
38. Margaret Fitzherbert, *Liberal Women: Federation to 1949*. Federation Press, Sydney, 2004 p. 182.
39. Sir James Killen, *Killen – Inside Australian Politics*, Methuen Haynes, North Ryde, 1985, p. 1.
40. Browne, *A Woman of Distinction*, pp. 41-2.
41. Ibid., p.47.
42. Management Newsletter, *Sixth in a Series on Federal Ministers*, Canberra, 28 March 1967, p. 9; NAA, Dame Annabelle Rankin-Press and biographical notes, 1971, M1569,47,1336240.
43. "Beauty and Wisdom In the Senate", *The Age*, Melbourne, 16 October 1947.
44. Senator Annabelle Rankin, "The Three Bears Will Growl Soon", *Courier-Mail*, 20 October 1947.

45 Senator Annabelle Rankin, "My Week In Parliament", *Courier-Mail*, 27 October 1947.
46 Oliver Hogue, "As One Woman to Another", *Sunday Sun and Guardian.* 26 October 1947.
47 Senator Annabelle Rankin, *Commonwealth Parliamentary Debates (CPD)*, Senate, 22 October 1947, pp. 1044-47.
48 Marion Saw and Marion Sims, *A Woman's Place; Women and Politics in Australia*, Allen and Unwin, Sydney, 1984, p. 46.
49 Rankin, *CPD*, Senate, 22 October 1947, pp. 1044-47.
50 Ibid.
51 Ibid.
52 Senator Neil O'Sullivan, *CPD*, Senate, 22 October 1947, p. 1048.
53 Senator Donald Cameron, *CPD*, Senate, 7 April 1948, pp. 575-6.
54 Senator Donald Cameron, *CPD*, Senate, 13 October 1948, p. 1485.
55 Senator Neil O'Sullivan and Senator Annabelle Rankin, and Senator Donald Cameron, *CPD*, Senate, 28 October, 1948, p. 2322.
56 Senator Neil O'Sullivan and Senator Annabelle Rankin, *CPD*, Senate, 28 October, 1948, pp. 2307-21.
57 Senator Annabelle Rankin, *CPD*, Senate, 22 June 1949, pp. 1255-7.
58 Ibid.
59 "Senator Rankin's Address to Women", *The Queensland Times*, 8 December 1949.
60 Charles Porter, *The 'Gut' Feeling*, Boolarong Publications, Brisbane, 1981, p. 15.
61 Senator Annabelle Rankin, "A Woman's View of Canberra", *Courier-Mail*, Brisbane, 27 February 1950.
62 NAA, ABC, op.cit – Enid Lyons.
63 Annabelle Rankin, *CPD*, Senate, 9 March 1950, p. 549.
64 Ibid., p. 550-2.
65 "Chivalry bid in Senate", *Courier-Mail*, 26 May 1950.
66 D.B. Waterson, O'Sullivan, Sir Michael Neil (1900-1968), *The Biographical Dictionary of the Senate*, https://biography.senate.gov.au/osullivan-michael-neil/
67 'Day by Day', *Courier-Mail*, 8 June 1950.
68 Parliamentary Education Office, Australian Parliament House.
69 Browne, *A Woman of Distinction*, p. 44.
70 Marchant, *Rankin, Dame Annabelle.*

71 Senator John Critchley, *CPD*, Senate, 6 June 1952, p. 1556.
72 NAA, ABC, op.cit. – Senator Ian Woods.
73 Hubert F. Opperman, *Pedals, Politics and People*, Haldane Publishing, Sydney, pp. 293-4.
74 *Brisbane Telegraph*, 19 September 1953.
75 Senator John Critchley, *CPD*, Senate, 30 September 1953, p. 357.
76 Ibid.
77 Senator Annabelle Rankin, *CPD*, Senate, 3 December 1953, pp. 358.
78 Browne, *A Woman of Distinction*, pp. 52-3.
79 Allan Martin, *Robert Menzies – A Life, Volume 2 1944-1978*, Melbourne University Press, Carlton, 1999, p. 246.
80 Browne, *A Woman of Distinction*.
81 The Queen's Speech, *CPD*, Senate, 15 February 1954, pp. 5-6.
82 Senator Annabelle Rankin, *CPD*, Senate, 28 September 1954, p. 546.
83 NAA, Folder of congratulatory messages maintained by Dame Annabelle Rankin, M2137,5,1141248.
84 Martin, *Robert Menzies*, p. 363.
85 Elgin Reid, "She kept the Senate going with 41 pins", *Courier-Mail*, 16 November 1957.
86 Martin, *Robert Menzies*, pp. 363-4.
87 Reid, "Sick Senators Start Battle of Nerves'" *Courier-Mail*, 30 November 1957.
88 Record of Senate vote, *CPD*, Senate, 27 November 1957, p. 1553.
89 Martin, *Robert Menzies*, p. 364.
90 Ian Hancock, *John Gorton – He did it his way*, Hodder Headline, Sydney, 2002, p. 81.
91 Senator Annabelle Rankin, *CPD*, Senate, 14 May 1963, pp. 416
92 Ibid., p. 418.
93 Senator Annabelle Rankin, *CPD*, Senate, 14 May 1963, pp. 416-9.
94 Martin, *Robert Menzies*, pp. 483-4.
95 Browne, *A Woman of Distinction*, p. 57.
96 Tom Frame, *The Life and Death of Harold Holt*, Allen and Unwin, Sydney, 2005, p. 161.
97 Management Newsletter, op.cit.,1967.
98 NAA, A Grant for Your Home, M2128, 29, 1336232.

99   Author's telephone conversation with Don Cameron, August 2022.
100   Clem Lloyd and Pat Troy, *Innovation and Reaction*, Allen and Unwin, Sydney, 1981, p. 10.
101   Senator Marie Breen, *CPD* Senate, 21 April 1966, pp. 477-501.
102   Senator Jim Cavanagh, *CPD*, Senate, 21 April 1966, pp. 477-8.
103   Senator McKenna, *CPD*, Senate, 5 May 1966, pp. 808-9.
104   Senator Annabelle Rankin, *CPD*, Senate, 5 May 1966, pp. 808-834.
105   The first, *Royal Commission on the Loss of HMAS Voyager*, was appointed by the Menzies Government and reported in 1964. Following criticisms, a second royal commission was appointed by the Holt Government in 1967.
106   Senator Annabelle Rankin, *CPD*, Senate, 18 April 1967, pp. 838-9.
107   NLA, Dame Annabelle Rankin, Oral History, Interview, op. cit.
108   NAA, Personal Papers of Prime Minister Holt, M2684,133,4681526.
109   NLA, Dame Annabelle Rankin, Oral History Interview, op. cit.
110   NLA, Dame Annabelle Rankin, Oral History Interview, op. cit.
111   NAA, Personal Papers of Prime Minister Holt, op. cit.
112   Ibid.
113   Ibid., p. 6.
114   NLA, Dame Annabelle Rankin, Oral History, op. cit.
115   Senator Annabelle Rankin, *CPD*, Senate, 13 June 1968, p. 1808.
116   Browne, *A Woman of Distinction*, p. 67.
117   Treasurer's Speech, Budget Speech, *CPD*, Senate, 12 August 1969, p. 43.
118   Senator Annabelle Rankin, *CPD*, Senate, 1 September 1970, pp. 364-5.
119   Patrick Mullins, *Tiberius with a telephone – The life and stories of William McMahon*, Scribe Publications, Melbourne, 2020, p. 406.
120   Senator the Honourable Dame Annabelle Rankin's resignation from the Senate, NAA, A11467, 31, 4034108. Her letter was sent to the G-G as the President of the Senate was away
121   Mullins, *Tiberuius with a telephone*, p. 406.
122   Senator Condon Byrne, *CPD*, Senate, 12 May 1971, p. 1716.
123   NAA, ABC transcript
124   Browne, *A Woman of Distinction*, p. 70.
125   NAA, ABC, op.cit. – John Melhuish.
126   Prime Minister Bob Hawke, *CPD*, House of Representatives, 16 September, 1986, p. 703.
127   Opposition Leader John Howard, *CPD*, Ibid.

www.ingramcontent.com/pod-product-compliance
Lightning Source LLC
Chambersburg PA
CBHW071414160426
43195CB00029B/2067